CELEBRATION OF A CENTENARY

COMMEMORATIVE BOOK AND CALENDAR OF EVENTS IN BIRMINGHAM 1989

*"Probably in no other
age or country was there
ever such an astonishing display
of human ingenuity as may be
found in Birmingham"*

ROBERT SOUTHEY, POET, 1807

First published — 17th November 1988. Published on behalf of Birmingham City Council by New Enterprise Publications Limited, 212 Broad Street, Birmingham B15 1AY
Designed by Three's Company Limited, 419 Stratford Road, Solihull B90 4AA. Phototypesetting by Typestyle (Birmingham) Limited, 34 Vittoria Street, Birmingham B1 3PE
Printed by Kings Norton Press Limited, Oxleasow Road, Redditch B98 0RE. ©Birmingham City Council. All rights reserved.

INDEX

Birmingham has experienced major social and economic change since 1889, but I am confident that the spirit of enterprise and concern for the community which has marked the efforts of the people of Birmingham over the last hundred years is still flourishing today.

This Centenary Souvenir Book contains an impressive programme of events and activities which I believe will appeal to all sections of the community. I am sure that the Centenary Year will provide the opportunity for all Birmingham's citizens to celebrate the achievements of their great City and to look forward with pride and optimism to the next Century of growth and vitality.

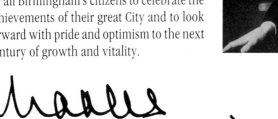

MESSAGE FROM COUNCILLOR HAROLD BLUMENTHAL, LORD MAYOR OF BIRMINGHAM

1989 will be a year when we can look back over a century of achievement. During the last 100 years the people of Birmingham have established themselves as great innovators who have turned their ideas into products and services and exported them to all corners of the world. It is particularly pleasing, therefore, that this Centenary Souvenir Book tells the story of Birmingham's successes. Birmingham is not just a city of the past though, it can, I am sure, look forward to another 100 years of enterprise and innovation and there are numerous exciting initiatives being undertaken by the present citizens of Birmingham in preparation for the next century.

Any birthday is about enjoyment, but 100th birthdays, of course, are a major cause for celebration. I feel sure that the wide range of activities illustrated in the calendar of events in this book will enable everyone to share in celebrating this important landmark in the history of our city.

The response from the Community to the City's Centenary has been overwhelming, and many of the Festival events have been suggested and are being organised by the people of Birmingham themselves, further demonstrating their drive and enthusiasm. I would like to thank all of them, and everyone else who has contributed to what I know will be a tremendous year and one that will be remembered for years to come.

Harold Blumenthal

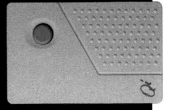

CADBURY'S FAVOURITE CENTRE FOR 100 YEARS.

THE BOURNVILLE FACTORY c.1889

In 1889, when Birmingham became a City, *Cadbury Brothers* was already a flourishing family business. Bournville, the company's home set in rolling fields four miles from the City, was known as the "factory in a garden."

1905

When *Cadbury's* Dairy Milk was introduced in 1905, its richness of taste and smoothness of texture were unrivalled and it is still, today, the most popular moulded chocolate bar in the UK. Many other favourites have been added over the years and Wispa is one of the latest success stories – it is an amazing fact

Just as memorable is *Cadbury's* advertising through the years – as consistent and classic as the brands themselves and always highlighting the quality and excellence of one of Britain's best loved treats.

THE HEADQUARTERS OF CADBURY LIMITED
1988

Today, the Bournville factory is amongst the largest and most modern of its kind in the world. Bristling with the latest technology, it works at truly awe-inspiring speeds, wrapping chocolate bars, for example, at the rate of 800 a minute – all to ensure that no-one misses out on their favourite chocolate.

RICHARD CADBURY
1835-1899

GEORGE CADBURY
1839-1922

At this time, the Company was run by *Richard* and *George Cadbury*, sons of the founder. The brothers must take the credit for making *Cadbury* the first name in chocolate even in those early days.

They constantly improved production techniques and quality, setting standards which made *Cadbury* famous worldwide.

that if all the Wispa bars eaten in a year were laid end to end, they would stretch round the world almost three times!

Creme Eggs can lay claim to equally startling statistics. Over 300 million a year are made – stacked one on top of the other, they would be ten times taller than Mount Everest.

c.1900

Cadbury look forward to another century of progress with the CITY OF BIRMINGHAM.

CADBURY CELEBRATES THE • CITY OF BIRMINGHAM CENTENARY FESTIVAL 1889 1989 • BIRMINGHAM CENTENARY

The First Name in Chocolate

Centenary City.

100 years of city, over 1000 years of history.

When Birmingham became a city on January 14, 1889, it marked the high point of achievement for the people who had campaigned for its improvement.

For only half a century had passed since the fledgling city had been but the remnant of

a feudal manor, struggling to establish good roads, water supply, drainage, housing and law and order.

The first step on the road to modern local government came in 1838 when Birmingham became a borough, which gave the Mayor and Council control over policing and the administration of justice.

TOP LEFT. VICTORIA BY THE GRACE OF GOD, QUEEN — THE CITY CHARTER, GRANTED JANUARY 14, 1889 TO THE LARGEST BOROUGH IN GREAT BRITAIN.

TOP RIGHT. THE BEGINNING — THE FIRST FORMAL MOVES TOWARDS LAW AND ORDER WITH THE STREET COMMISSION ACT, 1769.

RIGHT. THE FIRST STEP ALONG THE ROAD TO BECOMING BRITAIN'S SECOND CITY — THE BIRMINGHAM BOROUGH CHARTER, 1838.

LEFT. FORWARD, 1889 — THE FIRST COAT OF ARMS.

Until then, it had not even officially been a town, just a manorial organisation under the seal of Lord Birmingham and was only given parish status in 1708.

Such local government as existed was fragmentary; a Court Baron made bye-laws and transacted local government, while a Court Leet had some judicial powers.

The parishes were responsible for poor relief.

Some organisation had come in 1769 with the establishment of a Birmingham Street Commission to make up and maintain roads and sewers, with the power to levy rates.

This commission only acted in the parish of Birmingham, but it was followed by other commissions in the neighbouring parishes.

The Street Commissions were not incorporated into the rest of the local government organisation until 1852, while another 40 years were to pass before all the accepted responsibilities of a modern local authority were to be vested in one organisation.

Birmingham gained the status of a county borough in 1888 to separate itself from Warwickshire, and gained the right to call its senior citizen and chief magistrate the Lord Mayor in 1896.

Only one major landmark remained, and that was reached in 1905 when the Bishop of Worcester, Charles Gore, pledged his personal fortune to help found the diocese of Birmingham and he became the city's first bishop, naming St. Philip's Church as his cathedral.

Birmingham's power and influence in the region, the country and the world were already well-recognised in 1889.

The city's thousand manufacturing trades lay at the heart of its fame and prosperity, but it was as a market town that Birmingham first came to prominence in the Middle Ages.

The absentee lord of the manor, Peter de Bermingham, purchased a market charter from the Crown sometime between 1154 and 1166.

The charter gave the right to hold a market every Thursday, and it was the first regular market to be held in the area.

A later charter established an annual fair.

By getting in ahead of the surrounding towns, the manorial lord laid the foundations of enterprise for which the city gained worldwide respect.

The market may have been in unofficial existence before the charter, but the official document allowed the manor to levy charges and the market was an important source of income, for the farmland in the manor was poor.

The Domesday rolls of 1086 show Birmingham was one of the poorest manors in Warwickshire and worth only £1 compared with £4 for Sutton, and Aston, Handsworth and Yardley were worth £5 each.

Birmingham's origins are Anglo-Saxon, the name means the homestead (ham) of the family (ing) of Beorma (or Birm).

The manor was situated on a well-drained outcrop of sandstone, above the surrounding farmland and on the watershed of a number of small rivers.

In the valley below, the ford of Deritend over the River Rea was a focal point for local roads, and the early community grew in this area.

All around were the forests and farmlands of Staffordshire and Warwickshire which were to provide the raw materials of the future city's prosperity.

The market and the establishment of tanning and fulling mills on the River Rea helped the population to grow, from the 50 of Domesday to 1,500 in Tudor times.

By 1400 it was the third most wealthy place in Warwickshire.

Birmingham's parish church, St. Martin's in the Bull Ring, was established around this time though its foundation may date back to the Normans.

It certainly formed the nucleus of the market community and to this day, much rebuilt and extended, St. Martin's, rather than the newer St. Philip's Cathedral, is the church where the annual Civic Service is held to commemorate the incoming Lord Mayor.

The market and the de Bermingham's rule, which allowed many freedoms from the restrictive practices of the trade guilds of Coventry and elsewhere, encouraged newcomers.

The Lords of the Manor retained control of the markets until 1807, when the Street Commissioners acquired the lease, followed in 1824 by purchasing the rights.

In 1889, Victorian municipal enterprise was nearing its zenith, with only public transport, municipal housing and education to follow as cornerstones of the 20th Century city.

The city of 1889 included only the parishes of Birmingham, Edgbaston, Bordesley, Duddeston and Nechells.

The first expansion came in 1891, taking in Harborne, Balsall Heath, Saltley and Little Bromwich.

In 1911 came the biggest extension of the city, adding Northfield, King's Norton, Yardley, Handsworth, Erdington and Aston.

▷

TOP LEFT. CHARLES GORE, BISHOP OF WORCESTER, WHO PLEDGED HIS PERSONAL FORTUNE TO HELP FOUND THE DIOCESE OF BIRMINGHAM AND BECAME THE FIRST BISHOP, 1905.

TOP RIGHT. HANDSWORTH, 1859 – HAYMAKING IN MATTHEW'S FIELD, BY WILLIAM ELLIS. REPRODUCED BY PERMISSION OF THE BIRMINGHAM MUSEUM AND ART GALLERY.

CENTRE. HUB OF THE CITY – ST. MARTINS, PARISH CHURCH OF BIRMINGHAM, THE BULL RING AND HIGH STREET MARKETS.

BOTTOM LEFT. DOMESDAY 1086, WHEN BIRMINGHAM WAS WORTH JUST £1 (PUBLIC RECORDS OFFICE).

BOTTOM RIGHT. THE CHIEF MAGISTRATE BECOMES LORD MAYOR, 1896 – SIR JAMES SMITH, KT, IS THE FIRST IN OFFICE.

The most recent addition, in 1974, was the Royal Borough of Sutton Coldfield.

By 1889 most of the city's major public buildings were in place.

Most prominent, the Town Hall of 1834, the design by Joseph Hansom based on the Temple of Castor and Pollux in Rome, and the Council House, opened in 1879.

The founding father of the City of

ABOVE. THE TOWN HALL, BY JOSEPH HANSOM, MODELLED ON A ROMAN TEMPLE, SCENE OF CONCERTS AND PUBLIC MEETINGS.

FAR RIGHT. PIONEERS – THOMAS ATTWOOD, REFORMER AND FIRST MP, GEORGE DAWSON FOUNDER OF THE CIVIC GOSPEL, DR. ROBERT DALE, CARRS LANE MINISTER AND ADVOCATE OF MUNICIPAL IMPROVEMENT.

RIGHT. BRUMMAGEM JOE CHAMBERLAIN – POLITICIAN AND STATESMAN, WITH HIS THIRD WIFE, MARY ENDICOTT, THE FOUR SHARE A GRAVE IN KEY HILL.

Birmingham, Joseph Chamberlain, was by 1889 one of the city's Members of Parliament.

Neville Chamberlain, second son of Joseph, was to become another famous national politician as Prime Minister from 1937 to 1940.

Joseph was one of a number of nonconformists who campaigned for improvement and entered the Council in

1868 at a time when power was in the hands of economists, who had done little towards improving the town.

By 1874 he had made enough from his business interests to be able to devote himself to politics and in 1876 became one of the town's two MPs, joining John Bright on the radical wing of the Liberal Party.

When he left for national politics in 1883, he could claim the town had been "parked,

paved, assized, marketed, gas-and-watered and improved."

Indeed, when he became mayor in 1873, Joseph Chamberlain had declared: "The town shall not, with God's help, know itself."

Under Chamberlain came the great municipal age of expansion, with gas and water taken into local authority control, and the City Art Gallery erected over the offices of the gas department, paid for with its profits.

Chamberlain also began the great improvement of the squalid inner city which became Corporation Street, considered to be the first urban renewal scheme.

He was one of the first from Victorian local government to rise to national prominence, becoming Colonial Secretary in Gladstone's government.

But he was by no means the first from Birmingham to champion radical causes.

Men like Thomas Attwood advocated the cause of currency reform and universal

manhood suffrage, becoming the first Birmingham MP, and George Dixon gave up his parliamentary seat to Chamberlain to champion universal free education, along with the nonconformist preachers Dr. Robert Dale and George Dawson.

It was Dawson who created the concept of the Civic Gospel, the proposition that the town has a duty to its citizens and its prominent people have a public duty to guide that provision.

Dawson was disbarred from entering politics because he was a cleric, but his gospel was taken up by Chamberlain and other Victorian reformers to create the city state which Birmingham and other towns became.

Before them even came men like Joseph Priestley, the discoverer of oxygen whose radical ideas had led to the infamous riots of 1791, which culminated in the burning of his house, and in his emigration to the United States.

Birmingham's manufacturing base had been pioneered by the unknown men who set up blade mills, foundries and forges along its rivers. The blade mills provided the Parliamentary army with its swords, and provided the Royalist Prince Rupert with the reason to destroy them after a battle in 1643.

Steel furnaces set up in the area of the modern Steelhouse Lane provided the raw materials for a major industry, the manufacture of toys or ornaments.

Indeed, Birmingham's manufacturers became adept at converting the cheap raw materials of Staffordshire into more easily transportable and higher value goods, which helped to overcome the high cost of transport over poor roads.

The coming first of the canals in the 1760s and then the railways in the 1830s dramatically cut the transport costs and hastened the growth of heavier industry.

Birmingham became the centre first of the canal network, then the railway system, long before in the 1970s it became the focal point of the national Motorway network.

Brass, guns, jewellery and buttons became the staple of Birmingham industry, and local men patented cast-iron holloware, steel pen nibs, papier mache and screwcutting machines.

Industry demanded capital, which led to the foundation of banks and a Stock Exchange.

Industry also demanded literacy and

numeracy, and in 1830 surveys showed more than half the population could not sign their names, a situation hardly improved by 1869 when half the artisans could not read a newspaper.

Teacher training was an early reform, with the establishment of Saltley Training College in 1850, while after 1871 a school board provided a free place for every child and the King Edward's School Foundation set up six secondary schools, three for girls.

In higher education the pen manufacturer Josiah Mason gave his wealth

to open a science college in 1880 which formed the basis of Birmingham University, founded in 1900.

The Birmingham and Midland Institute pioneered science classes and its technical school was taken over by the Council which opened the Municipal Technical School in 1891.

The culmination was the foundation in 1956 of the country's first College of Advanced Technology in Corporation Street, the nucleus of the present day Aston University, which received its charter in 1966.

▷

TOP LEFT. X THE SIGNATURE OF LITERACY... ST. MARTIN'S REGISTER, 1836.

TOP RIGHT. BIRMINGHAM UNIVERSITY, FOUNDED AROUND JOSIAH MASON'S SCIENCE COLLEGE AND THE BIRMINGHAM MEDICAL SCHOOL IN 1900, AND THE LAST OF JOSEPH CHAMBERLAIN'S GREAT UNDERTAKINGS, COMMEMORATED WITH CHAMBERLAIN TOWER, LANDMARK FOR A CITY.

CENTRE. EDUCATION 1896.

BELOW. EDUCATION 1989.

The city's first public libraries opened in 1866, the Central Reference Library and the Deritend branch library opening on the same day.

Today's Central Library is the largest in Europe.

Public health, water supply and sewerage were the focus of civic attention in the early 19th Century, but the early Borough Council was slow to improve facilities.

Not until the Chamberlain era were the problems solved.

Later developments saw Birmingham build the Elan Valley reservoir and aqueduct, extracting water from the Welsh mountains, opened by King Edward VII in 1904.

The markets which formed the original nucleus of the city's commerce came under the control of the Council in 1851, and at that time were still largely in the streets around the Bull Ring as well as in the Market Hall which was built in 1835.

Special meat, fish and vegetable markets were built together with an abattoir, and post-war development culminated in the construction of a modern wholesale markets complex, formally opened in 1976.

Housing was largely a matter for private developers in the Victorian era, though the Council could control the type of construction and banned the back-to-back and courtyard housing which rapidly became insanitary.

The 1909 Town Planning Act gave the first real controls over development and led to the establishment of municipal housing.

At its peak the Council owned 38 per cent of the city's housing.

Transport in the city was largely based on railways and horse buses until the 1870s when first horse and then steam tramways were established.

The Council instituted a policy of constructing the lines and leasing them to private operators, but in 1904 started operating its own electric trams.

Motor buses followed in 1913, the trams and buses were extended into the new housing estates in the suburbs.

Electric trams provided a firm market for the city's electricity supply department which built power stations at Nechells and Hams Hall, nationalised in 1948.

The First World War saw the beginning of Britain's first municipal bank, when the Lord Mayor, Neville Chamberlain, launched a savings scheme which guaranteed interest on investments.

The scheme became the Birmingham Municipal Bank in 1919; the bank became part of the Trustee Savings Bank, now operated as a public company by TSB plc.

Social provisions in the city had been part of Dawson's Civic Gospel, but the Great War also saw the formation of the Birmingham

Citizens' Committee to administer welfare.

The first rationing scheme in Britain began in July 1917 when the Birmingham Cooperative Society started a sugar ration, six months ahead of Government food policy.

The bombing during the Second World War and the subsequent Town and Country Planning Act gave the impetus to redevelopment.

Birmingham was one of the first to be granted an Inner City Partnership which in conjunction with the Government is responsible for urban regeneration.

Local government has changed in the hundred years since Birmingham became a city, and the City Council has adapted to those changes.

In 1974 the City Council lost many of its departments and powers, handing over water supply and sewerage to the Severn Trent Water Authority and highways, public transport, police and fire services to the West Midlands County Council.

That body was abolished in 1986, but the former County Council services are now administered by joint boards of the seven district councils in its area.

The 150th anniversary of the Borough of Birmingham in 1988 saw the launch of a major initiative in the spirit of Joseph Chamberlain's Corporation Street development.

Birmingham Heartlands is a project designed to rejuvenate one of the city's most run-down areas covering Aston, Nechells, Duddeston, Bordesley and parts of Bromford, beginning where Corporation Street ends.

It is Britain's first private venture development corporation, bringing together the City Council, the Chamber of Industry and Commerce, and a consortium of private contractors.

Before the year 2000 the Heartlands project will clear up the desolation left from wartime bombing, factory closures and general urban rundown.

New homes and factories will be developed, while upgrading and improving existing property, helping to build perhaps 3,000 new houses and create 12,000 new jobs.

The Heartlands project will also have a rapid transit link with a line of the planned Midland Metro network, whose first line will run from Snow Hill through the Black Country to Wolverhampton by 1992.

The Council is also directly involved in the economic regeneration of the city, with a wide range of measures to stimulate business and encourage development.

The National Exhibition Centre at Bickenhill which opened in 1976 is a joint venture by the city and industry, and is now one of the busiest exhibition complexes in Europe.

The Council has a wide range of initiatives to encourage industrial development, from the traditional to the new technologies, and Aston Science Park is a project set up with Aston University and Lloyds Bank to foster new science-based industry.

It also sees tourism and leisure

It is being followed by the development of the International Convention Centre, close to the city centre, which will open in 1991 and incorporate a conference centre, concert hall and an indoor sports arena.

One of the first meetings at the centre will be of the International Olympic Committee, and the major political parties are also considering it as an alternative to their usual seaside venues.

developments as a priority, and events like the annual Halfords Birmingham Super Prix, Britain's only on-the-streets motor race, help to maintain a reputation for innovation. ◇ ◇

TOP RIGHT. SNOW HILL, ONCE THE GATEWAY TO LONDON AND THE WEST COUNTRY, CLOSED, RAZED, REDEVELOPED FOR OFFICES AND THE STATION REOPENED TO IMPROVE COMMUNICATIONS.

ABOVE. INTERNATIONAL SHOWPLACE – THE NATIONAL EXHIBITION CENTRE.

TOP LEFT. WAR HITS BIRMINGHAM – BOMB CRATERS IN BULL STREET, CHILDREN EVACUATED.

Premier Brands
congratulates The City of Birmingham on its 100th Birthday.

Premier Brands Ltd., P.O. Box 171, Birmingham B30 2NA

* Under licence from Cadbury Schweppes plc

PREMIER
BRANDS

RACKHAMS, PART OF THE FABRIC OF OUR GREAT CITY

1 8 8 9 ———————— 1 9 8 9

BIRMINGHAM

Corporation Street, Birmingham B2 5JS. Tel: 021-236 3333.

YOUR LOCAL HOUSE OF FRASER STORE

WE'VE BEEN SOMETHING IN THE CITY FOR 100 YEARS

BRITANNIC ASSURANCE, MOOR GREEN, MOSELEY, BIRMINGHAM B13 8QF.

LIFE ASSURANCE · PENSIONS · UNIT LINKED INVESTMENTS · HOME AND MOTOR INSURANCE · MORTGAGES · SAVINGS

*F*or over 85 years the privately owned, independent family business of Lee Longlands has graced the city skyline, offering the more discerning homemaker a wide and exclusive selection of high quality furniture and furnishings with that touch of individuality.

'Darracq Delivery Van: Circa 1912'

Starting in those early days from their first premises in Broad Street, opposite where the Hall of Memory stands today, residents in Edgbaston were quick to appreciate the excellence. With the inherent desire to supply quality, stylish furniture, extensive Cabinet workshops were set up at the rear of the premises; demand increased and it wasn't long before the horse drawn delivery vans were replaced with a Darracq van to cope with deliveries further afield.

'Original Premises in 1903 (opposite present Hall of Memory)

"Stylish sophistication timeless elegance."

*T*oday Lee Longlands are located half way along Broad Street in their own distinctively styled building. Once inside you'll discover shopping with a difference. A personal service in a relaxing environment.

There's a wealth of high quality, distinctively styled furnishings which combine excellent craftsmanship with superb design, both modern and traditional, with outstanding value for money.

You'll find Furniture and Lighting from all over the world. One of the finest carpet and oriental rug departments in the Midlands, a fabulous selection of upholstery from British designers and craftsmen and an International collection of curtain fabrics and linens. Also there's a full Interior Design Service, new Bathroom and Kitchen Showrooms and so much more.

Between departments you can pause in our pleasant Coffee Lounge whilst the children play happily and safely in the 'Rumpus Room'.

Experience personal shopping as it ought to be. Lee Longlands.

'The showrooms today'

LEE LONGLANDS
CLASSIC STYLE. CLASSIC STORE.

oad Street Birmingham B15 1AU 021-643 9101
Open 6 days a week Customer Car Park at rear

OUR BRAND NEW TELEPHONE NETWORK FEEDS ON FIBRE. NO WONDER IT'S SO HEALTHY.

The first thing people notice about the Mercury network is how clear the lines are.

The reason's simple. Since 1983, we've laid over 20,000 kilometres of optical fibre cable across Britain, so your calls arrive in perfect shape.

Now that's got to be healthy development.

To hear more, contact

**Mercury Communications Ltd,
Midlands Regional Office,
Alpha Tower,
Suffolk Street Queensway,
Birmingham B1 1TT
021-625 2000**

Mercury
COMMUNICATIONS

Mercury Communications is a member of the Cable and Wireless Worldwide Communications Group

We helped
make it faster.

Jaguar's renowned engines used to lose speed on the production line because engine blocks had to be cleaned and dried by hand. It was time-consuming and unpleasant.

Now, thanks to the Air Knife which was developed at MEB's Power Technology Centre, engine block decontamination speed has been increased by a massive 60 per cent.

Because the whole process was automated it also improved working conditions and costs.

The Air Knife, a fan driven machine discharging a thin blade of high velocity air for cleaning and drying, is just one typical example of the work carried out at MEB Power Technology Centre. Our expertise also extends to metal melting, infra-red heating and induction heating.

Since 1958, we've helped hundreds of companies, at home and abroad, to solve problems and find more efficient ways of using electricity.

Today MEB provide a vital service for nearly two million customers in the domestic, industrial, commercial, agricultural and public sectors.

Including making Jaguar faster.

POWER FOR THE HEART OF BRITAIN

City of entertainment.

Birmingham, centre stage for the world.

A visitor to Birmingham in 1846 remarked that, if most towns could be said to show a cultural speciality of one kind or another, it was the love of music which singled out Birmingham.

His theory was that music filled the vacuum left when the forges stopped ringing at the end of the day. True or not, Birmingham can certainly claim a long and distinguished musical tradition focused initially on the Triennial Music Festival which began in the 18th Century and ran until 1912.

Mendelssohn composed his oratorio, Elijah, for the festival in 1846. Between then and 1912, when Sibelius conducted the British premiere of his Fourth Symphony, a succession of distinguished composers visited Birmingham, often paying tribute to the musicality of the natives. "I wish people who describe the English as unmusical could hear the Birmingham singers...they certainly perform as if they were the finest musicians in the world", wrote Saint-Saens. Dvorak, who composed his Requiem for Birmingham, wrote home: "I'm here in this immense industrial city, where they make excellent knives, scissors, springs, files and goodness knows what else, and, besides these, music too. And how well! It's terrifying how much the people here manage to achieve!"

The young Edward Elgar played in the orchestra conducted by Dvorak, and his own oratorios, The Dream of Gerontius, The Apostles and The Kingdom, were composed for the festival. Elgar had a close association with the city: he was the first professor of music at Birmingham University and conducted the inaugural concert by the City of Birmingham Orchestra (it added the "Symphony" much later) in 1920.

Birmingham's first theatre opened in Moor Street in 1740, and theatre developed along with the city throughout the 19th Century.

But Birmingham's most famous contribution to the history of theatre came with the founding of the Repertory Theatre in Station Street in 1913. This pioneering institution owed its origins to the vision and personal fortune of Sir Barry Jackson, and

developed out of an amateur company, the Pilgrim Players.

During the 1920s the Rep staged a series of celebrated productions including Back to Methuselah by Jackson's friend George Bernard Shaw (when Jackson told Shaw of his intention to stage this epic, the author's solemn reaction was: "Mr Jackson, are your wife and children provided for?") and The Immortal Hour, the opera by Rutland Boughton which became a smash-hit in London but has sadly not stood the test of time.

Many of the Rep's ventures were met with apathy by the Birmingham public, and Jackson threatened to uproot the company. Fortunately he relented, and the Rep went on

ABOVE. SIR EDWARD ELGAR, THE WORCESTERSHIRE-BORN COMPOSER WHOSE CAREER HAD MANY LINKS WITH BIRMINGHAM, INCLUDING THE COMPOSITION OF THE DREAM OF GERONTIUS FOR THE 1900 MUSIC FESTIVAL.

TOP RIGHT. CEDRIC HARDWICK AND EDITH EVANS IN BIRMINGHAM REPERTORY THEATRE'S 1923 PREMIERE OF SHAW'S BACK TO METHUSELAH, PLUS SHAW WITH THE CAST OF BACK TO METHUSELAH.

BOTTOM RIGHT. THEATRE ROYAL PLAYBILLS, 1888.

to establish a unique reputation in British theatre for the distinguished roll-call of actors — including Laurence Olivier, Paul Scofield, Albert Finney and Derek Jacobi — who gained their early experience there.

The Rep moved from Station Street to a new building in Broad Street in 1971. The Old Rep, as it is now known, survives as a venue for amateur companies. The amateur theatre

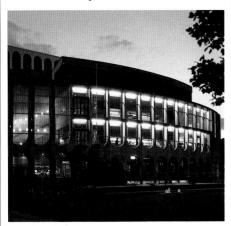

scene continues to thrive, with leading companies like the Crescent, with its city-centre theatre built in the 1960s, and the Hall Green and Highbury Little Theatres.

Among Birmingham's lost theatres the Theatre Royal in New Street, built as early as 1774 and demolished in 1956, was particularly long-lamented. Two old theatres which survive are the Alexandra (opened in 1901) and the Hippodrome (1899). The Alex was run for many years by the Salberg family, Birmingham's best known theatrical dynasty. It is held in special affection by the Birmingham public, of which it draws a wide

cross-section, not least for its traditional Christmas pantomimes. It had its own repertory company as late as the mid-70's but now specialises in touring drama.

The Hippodrome had to wait more than 80 years to enjoy its most prestigious era. Originally a variety theatre (Charlie Chaplin was among the performers to appear there during its early days), it had become run-down and near-redundant by 1979, when it was bought by the city and taken over by a newly-created trust.

In a two-phase redevelopment the stage was doubled in depth, opening up the theatre to major opera and ballet companies. The world's largest, the Kirov Opera, visited the Hippodrome on its first British tour in 1987. Now part of a national circuit of newly-restored Victorian lyric theatres, the Hippodrome is recognised as one of Britain's leading venues for opera, ballet and musical spectaculars.　　　　　▷

TOP LEFT. LEONARD BERNSTEIN'S CANDIDE, STAGED BY THE BIRMINGHAM REPERTORY THEATRE AT THE EDINBURGH FESTIVAL.

BOTTOM LEFT. THE NEW BIRMINGHAM REPERTORY THEATRE, WHICH OPENED IN 1971.

TOP RIGHT. THE THEATRE ROYAL, NEW STREET, 1774-1956.

BOTTOM RIGHT. THE BIRMINGHAM HIPPODROME AFTER ITS REFURBISHMENT.

Many of the early efforts to provide Birmingham with a cultural dimension in the 19th Century focused on the Birmingham and Midland Institute, founded in 1854, which still survives as a cultural centre today, with its library and programmes of concerts, talks and exhibitions.

ABOVE. THE CANNON HILL PUPPET THEATRE HAS BEEN A DISTINGUISHED INGREDIENT OF THE MIDLANDS ARTS CENTRE SINCE IT OPENED IN 1962.

TOP RIGHT. BBC PEBBLE MILL STUDIOS, EDGBASTON.

BOTTOM RIGHT. A WATERCOLOUR BY DAVID COX (1783-1859), ONE OF THE MOST DISTINGUISHED ARTISTS TO BE BORN IN BIRMINGHAM.

The post-1945 era brought new kinds of arts institutions. The Midlands Arts Centre, opened in 1962, was an ambitious concept housing a wide range of artistic activity, from performance to practical classes, in a single complex within Cannon Hill Park. Like the Rep, it was largely the vision of one man, John English, who also had a background in amateur theatre in the city.

Today the arts centre has moved some way from the original concept of an educational centre aimed primarily at children and young people. But one common factor throughout its history has been the Cannon Hill Puppet Theatre, directed by the internationally-acclaimed puppeteer, John Blundall.

Cinema exhibition in Birmingham began with "biograph" inserts into music hall programmes. Possibly the city's first purpose-built cinema was the Electric Theatre in Station Street (1910).

The film pioneer G. B. Samuelson was briefly involved in production before the First World War, but otherwise Birmingham did not establish itself as a centre for film-making, except much later for television. In the last few years there have been moves to remedy this, associated with the city's Film and Television Festival.

Birmingham's two television studios, BBC Pebble Mill and Central (formerly ATV) both opened in the early 1970s. Central's best productions have tended to be in the field of documentary, whether local or international in scope. Particularly outstanding at Pebble Mill was the drama output in the 1970s under the direction of David Rose, which anticipated the influential Film on Four series he launched on moving to Channel 4 as its first commissioning editor for drama.

Birmingham produced two 19th Century painters of international status in the watercolourist David Cox (1783-1859) and

Sir Edward Burne-Jones (1833-1898). Unlike Cox, Burne-Jones did not return to live in his native city in later life, although two late masterpieces, The Star of Bethlehem (commissioned by the City) and the stained glass in Birmingham Cathedral, were produced for Birmingham. He was also a president of the Royal Birmingham Society of

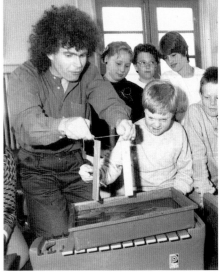

building on Great Charles Street.

A survey of the state of the Arts in Birmingham in its centenary year would have to conclude that music retains its traditional pre-eminence, above all through the spectacular recent success of the City of Birmingham Symphony Orchestra.

For most of its history the orchestra was essentially of local importance, despite the distinction of two of its early conductors, Adrian Boult and Leslie Heward. Horizons began to broaden in the 1970s under the French conductor Louis Fremaux, who founded the CBSO Chorus and began to record for EMI.

But the orchestra's meteoric rise began with the appointment of Simon Rattle, then aged 25, as principal conductor in 1980. Since then the orchestra has made its debut in a string of world centres including Paris, Berlin, Helsinki, Tokyo, Washington, New York and Boston. A growing list of recordings has spread the orchestra's name worldwide and it has enjoyed more exposure on British television than any other. A development plan, funded jointly by the Arts Council and

▷

Artists, which was founded as an exhibiting society for local artists early in the 19th Century and continues to fulfill this role today.

Burne-Jones's friend William Morris was an important influence on Birmingham through his utopian views on art and design, which formed the basis for the Arts and Crafts movement. The foundation of the Museum and Art Gallery (1885) followed a similar philosophy to that of the South Kensington Museum (later the Victoria & Albert), with the idea that access to examples of good design from around the world would inspire better design in Birmingham's products and make them more competitive: hence the applied art emphasis in the museum's collections.

The School of Art became a focal point for Birmingham's distinctive contribution to the Arts and Crafts movement around the turn of the century, encompassing a wide range of media including jewellery, metalwork, stained glass and book illustration. There was also a flowering of Arts and Crafts architecture and, despite the reckless demolition of some of its finest examples, much remains, including Arthur Dixon's Guild of Handicrafts

TOP LEFT. BIRMINGHAM MUSEUM AND ART GALLERY OPENED IN 1885.
THE FEENEY ART GALLERIES, IN THE COUNCIL HOUSE EXTENSION, WERE ADDED IN 1911.

RIGHT. SIMON RATTLE MEETS TOMORROW'S AUDIENCE AS PART OF THE CBSO'S "ADOPT-A-PLAYER" EDUCATIONAL SCHEME.

Birmingham City Council, could turn the orchestra into Britain's leading international contender and from 1991 it will have a concert hall designed to the highest standards within the International Convention Centre.

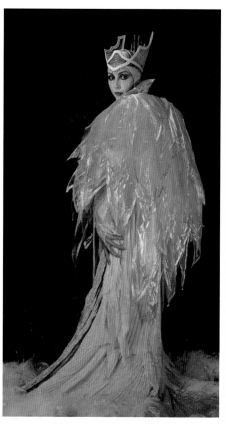

TOP LEFT. LEGENDARY BLUES SINGER MEMPHIS SLIM PERFORMING AT THE BIRMINGHAM INTERNATIONAL JAZZ FESTIVAL.

TOP RIGHT. THE SADLER'S WELLS ROYAL BALLET'S PRODUCTION OF THE SNOW QUEEN, WHICH HAD ITS PREMIERE AT BIRMINGHAM HIPPODROME.

RIGHT. CITY OF BIRMINGHAM TOURING OPERA IN ITS PRODUCTION OF VERDI'S FALSTAFF, WHICH TOURED BRITAIN DURING 1987-88

The importance of the Hippodrome as a centre for opera and ballet has already been mentioned. The theatre has particularly fruitful relationships with two companies who regard the theatre as their second home: Welsh National Opera and Sadler's Wells Royal Ballet.

The latter makes use of the Hippodrome's superior facilities to premiere all its major new productions in Birmingham, a development which in 1988 led to an invitation from the city and the theatre to the company to move its base to the city.

Music making continues to thrive at all levels. Birmingham's choral tradition, perhaps not sufficiently recognised outside the city, continues through such groups as the City of Birmingham Choir, Ex Cathedra, the Birmingham Festival Choral Society, the Choral Union and others. Birmingham also has its own recently-formed opera company, City of Birmingham Touring Opera, which works on a small scale but to the highest standards. Its projects have ranged from national tours of Verdi and Mozart to a rock-gospel opera produced in association with the community arts centre, The Cave, based in Balsall Heath.

The Birmingham Jazz Festival has helped put the city on the international jazz map in recent years, and Birmingham is established among the leading centres for the pop music world even though the scale of concerts has escalated over the last 20 years. Birmingham Town Hall was eclipsed as a venue first by the Odeon, New Street and then the National

Exhibition Centre, while for the 1988 Bruce Springsteen tour only Villa Park was big enough. Successful performers who have emerged from the city since the 1960s include The Move, Steve Winwood, Electric Light Orchestra, Joan Armatrading, Duran Duran and UB40.

Birmingham's three major theatres enter the city's second century in good health, and a mushroom growth of small scale, community-based theatre companies is an interesting recent development.

The contemporary visual arts are more patchily served. Ikon Gallery, founded in 1965 as a gallery for local artists, now provides a showcase for new work from throughout Britain, but the city's collections of 20th Century art are limited. The Museum and Art Gallery has ambitious plans to develop a large exhibition suite for temporary exhibitions, and this is surely a vital piece of the cultural jigsaw for a city with international ambitions.

Another recent development is a growing population of young artists who have joined together to lease studios in redundant industrial premises. But as Birmingham's economic recovery continues, space is at a premium, and some ingenuity may be needed to exploit the potential to make Birmingham a centre for living art. The work of contemporary artists is at least likely to become more familiar to the Birmingham public over the next few years, with commissions for the city streets and major developments like the International Convention Centre and the Brindley Place development.

Birmingham's multicultural character is likely to add a distinctive flavour to arts and entertainment in Birmingham as it approaches the 21st century. It can already boast one of Britain's leading Afro-Caribbean dance companies, Kokuma, which toured nationally during 1988.

There is plenty to build upon, but still some gaps that need to be filled as Birmingham seeks to establish itself as a true international meeting place. The city's plans for encouraging the development of a media industry — film, video, photography, design

— building on the services required by the convention centre, is one example of the new opportunities which may now arise, but it needs to act quickly and flexibly to make the most of them. If so, it could be an exciting next 100 years. ◇ ◇ ◇ ◇ ◇ ◇ ◇ ◇ ◇ ◇

FAR LEFT. IKON GALLERY PROVIDES A SHOWCASE FOR NEW DEVELOPMENTS IN THE VISUAL ARTS. THIS EXHIBITION EXPLORED THE CONTINUING ROMANTIC TRADITION IN BRITISH PAINTING.

LEFT. HANDSWORTH-BASED KOKUMA PERFORMING ARTS HAS ESTABLISHED ITSELF AS ONE OF BRITAIN'S LEADING COMPANIES SPECIALISING IN AFRO-CARIBBEAN DANCE.

BELOW. UB40 ACHIEVED INTERNATIONAL POPULARITY WHILE REFLECTING THE NEW MULTICULTURAL BIRMINGHAM.

THE INTERNATIONAL STOCK EXCHANGE

BIRMINGHAM MEMBER FIRMS

CHAMBERS & REMINGTON
Canterbury House, 85 Newhall Street, Birmingham B3 1LS.
Tel. No. 236 2577

FYSHE HORTON FINNEY & CO.
Charles House, 148/149 Great Charles Street,
Birmingham B3 3HT.
Tel. No. 236 3111

F.H.F. MARKET MAKERS LTD.
Charles House, 148/149 Great Charles Street,
Birmingham B3 3HT.
Tel. No. 236 2211

GRIFFITHS & LAMB
York House, 38 Great Charles Street, Queensway,
Birmingham B3 3AH.
Tel. No. 236 6641

HARRIS ALLDAY LEA & BROOKS
Stock Exchange Buildings, 33 Great Charles Street,
Queensway, Birmingham B3 3JN.
Tel. No. 233 1222

ROY JAMES & CO.
Stock Exchange Buildings, 33 Great Charles Street,
Queensway, Birmingham B3 3JS.
Tel. No. 200 2200

MARGETTS & ADDENBROOKE
York House, 38 Great Charles Street, Queensway,
Birmingham B3 3JU.
Tel. No. 200 2002

MURRAY & CO. STOCKBROKERS LTD.
Beaufort House, 96 Newhall Street, Birmingham B3 1PE.
Tel. No. 200 3377

I.A. PRITCHARD STOCKBROKERS LTD.
New Oxford House, 16 Waterloo Street, Birmingham.
Tel. No. 643 7877

SABIN BACON WHITE & CO.
6 The Wharf, Bridge Street, Birmingham.
Tel. No. 631 2292

ALBERT E. SHARP & CO.
Edmund House, 12/22 Newhall Street, Birmingham B3 3ER
Tel. No. 200 2244

SHARELINK LTD.
Edmund House, 10th Floor, 12/22 Newhall Street,
Birmingham B3 3ER.
Tel. No. 200 2242

SMITH KEEN CUTLER LTD.
Exchange Buildings, Stephenson Place, New Street,
Birmingham B2 4NN
Tel. No. 643 9977

STOCK BEECH & CO. LTD.
Lloyds Bank Chambers, 75 Edmund Street,
Birmingham B3 3HL.
Tel. No. 233 3211

THE STOCK EXCHANGE IN BIRMINGHAM 1845-1989
A MARKET FOR ALL SECURITIES

BIRMINGHAM
LAW SOCIETY

The legal heart of England for 170 years,
still beating strongly, with Solicitors providing
services to meet local,
national and international
requirements.

*Founded
in 1818*

8 Temple Street,
Birmingham B2 5BT.

Telephone: 021-643 9116
Fax: 021-633 3507

*T*he University of Birmingham owes its existence to the vision and generosity of the men and women of Birmingham. Now one of the country's leading centres of teaching and research, the University continues to enjoy close cultural and commercial links with the City.

THE UNIVERSITY OF BIRMINGHAM – FOR TEACHING AND RESEARCH

*T*he influence of the region has helped to make the University a leader in industrial and commercial research and collaboration. In addition to the full range of undergraduate and postgraduate degree and diploma courses, the University runs specially tailored courses to meet the needs of industry and commerce.

If you would like to know more about study and training at the University as an undergraduate, postgraduate or professional person, contact: *the Director of Public Affairs, University of Birmingham, P.O. Box 363, Birmingham B15 2TT.*

THE UNIVERSITY OF BIRMINGHAM – AS A CONFERENCE CENTRE

*T*he University has a wide range of accommodation and facilities for Conferences · Meetings · Seminars · Courses · Exhibitions · Group travel · Holiday flats.

CONFERENCES The University's distinctive red-brick buildings and its halls of residence are a perfect setting for conferences of all kinds. Intensive academic or professional conferences find the larger lecture theatres with full technical and audio-visual support ideal for their sessions. The large modern halls of residence in their beautiful parkland setting around a lake are peaceful and comfortable to return to in the evenings. Smaller conferences or special seminars can be completely self-contained in one of the Halls of Residence. Well-stocked bars and expert catering staff ensure that any social function from a sherry reception to a full-scale banquet can be provided.

MEETINGS The University can provide rooms of all sizes and varieties from 400-seat tiered lecture theatres to 16 person seminar rooms.

EXHIBITIONS The University's magnificent Great Hall has 900 square metres of floor area and most major lecture theatre complexes have rooms suitable for exhibitions adjoining.

SPECIAL COURSES The University has its own residential course and conference centre which is available all year. Built and furnished to a high standard the Lucas Institute is adjacent to the main campus in Edgbaston. It is particularly suited to companies or organisations wishing to run series of courses. Up to 40 delegates are accommodated in single study bedrooms with washbasins and tea and coffee facilities. For more information contact: *Mr Edward Farrar at the Conferences Office, telephone 021-454 6022.*

THE UNIVERSITY OF BIRMINGHAM – WORKING WITH INDUSTRY

BIRMINGHAM RESEARCH PARK

*T*he University of Birmingham Research Park is an 8 acre site in Edgbaston adjacent to the University campus and the Queen Elizabeth Medical Centre. It offers purpose-built accommodation or building plots to companies seeking to work with the University in research, development or training. The Research Park is a joint venture between Birmingham University and Birmingham City Council and companies there have access to support services from the City Council as well as to the sports, social and technical facilities of the University.

On the Research Park is the Institute of Research and Development, a multi-unit building providing 25,000 sq. ft. of high quality accommodation. Flexible tenancies are available for units from 350 sq. ft. upwards. It already houses a dozen companies involved in biotechnology, computer software, and other scientific developments.

One of these is Birmingham Research and Development Ltd, the University's technology transfer company. It helps companies to develop contacts with the 39 University departments in Science, Engineering and Medicine, with the City Council Business Development Service, and with sources of venture capital and professional advice. BRDL also offers industry world-wide access to the University's technology on a licensing basis. For more information, contact: *Dr Derek Burr at BRDL, telephone 021-471 4977.*

BACKWARD THINKING.

There's a rather clever touch on the new Rover Fastback.

If your front wipers are switched on and you engage reverse gear the rear wiper automatically clears your view at the back.

But surely, thoughtful touches like that only come on top of the range models, with price tags to match?

Not so. Just look at the Rover 820. Even a quick glance reveals just how painstaking Rover have been to guarantee your comfort. Closer inspection is even more rewarding.

Take the fascia for instance. Carefully selected burr walnut; over one hundred years old.

Space: 49.6 cu ft. (With rear seat down.)
Pace: 112 mph. (With right foot down.)

You'll also find care has been taken that night driving is as relaxing as possible.

All light sources, including the eight speaker radio and cassette illumination, are tuned to the same soft orange to reduce glare and be gentle on the eye.

Outside temperature is something you can never be sure of in this not-so temperate isle. The five thousand watt heater can take the inside temperature of the 820 from a bitter −20°C to +20°C in minutes.

But what of more obvious luxuries like electric front windows, central locking, remotely controlled door mirrors, tailgate release and fuel cap? All standard, on the 820.

While an electronic engine management system guarantees the smooth running of the economical but spirited 2 litre power unit.

And the price for all this attention to detail? Dare we say a mere £12,640?

Yes, we certainly do.

ROVER 800 SERIES

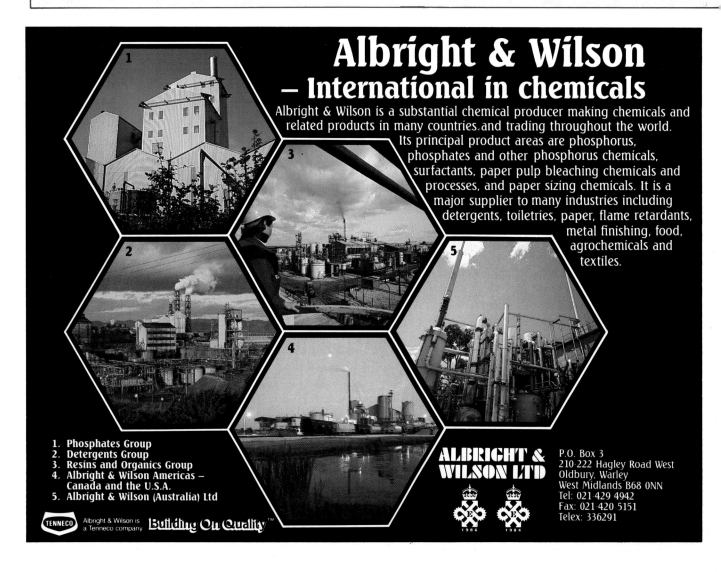

City of enterprise.

Birmingham, investing in the future.

A campaign which many would never have thought necessary is being fought by Birmingham City Council.

The campaign is to attract industry and commerce to set up and to expand in the city.

It is backed with a range of incentives which aim to counter the more financially attractive packages available in other parts of the country.

But its basic message is the message which attracted industry to Birmingham in the first place, central location, good transport links, raw materials and an enterprising workforce.

The city's founding fathers would perhaps ask why these advantages are not obvious for all to see, but they had never been faced with national policies which encouraged industry to move from its natural base.

TOP LEFT. EARLY MENTION OF BIRMINGHAM INDUSTRY, 1300.
RIGHT THE GROWING CITY – 1553.
ABOVE. COMMUNICATIONS CENTRE – TELECOM TOWER.

Nor had they been faced with the devastating results of world recession.

For, except in the aftermath of the Napoleonic Wars, Birmingham industry had not had to face serious structural recession.

Even the Hungry Thirties saw new technology, in the shape of the mass-produced car and the aeroplane, moving in to replace declining trades.

The commerce which was formalised in the 12th Century when Birmingham was granted a market charter is perhaps the starting point of its commercial success.

Its rivers flowed fast enough to encourage fullers, weavers, tanners and iron workers to set up mills to process the raw materials of Staffordshire and Warwickshire into saleable goods.

Henry VIII's commissioner John Leland, appointed to report on the state of the country to the Tudor monarch, wrote in 1536 of the "smithies, naylors and cutlers of Direty (Deritend)."

Leland described the bridges across the River Rea, and of walking up the "mene hill" into Birmingham, where the smithies made

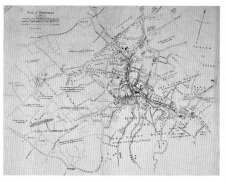

knives "and all manner of cuttynge tools and lorimars that make byts and a great many naylors. So that a great part of the towne is mayntayned by smithies having yren out of Staffordshire and Warwickshire and see cole out of Staffordshire."

Leland's tour came as Henry was dissolving the monasteries after his break with Rome, and three years after the de Berminghams had forfeit their manorial rights, putting more power and freedom into the hands of the people.

This freedom proved an attraction for those trying to escape the restrictive practices of trade guilds of older towns like Coventry.

A hundred years after Leland, Birmingham forges supplied the Parliamentary Army with 15,000 swords, a streak of independence which brought the wrath of the Royalists upon them, and Royalist forces plundered the town and destroyed some of the mills.

The Stuart period saw the establishment of Birmingham's gun trade and by 1690

Birmingham gunsmiths were contracted to provide 200 muskets a month to the Government.

So important did the trade become that in 1813, at the height of the Napoleonic Wars, the town gained its own gun barrel Proof House, so cutting the costs of sending every barrel to London for testing and approval.

Birmingham supplied two thirds of the firearms to the Army and Navy during that war: the trade recession that followed the end of hostilities was the last to affect the town dramatically until 1981.

The gun trade, with its specialist craftsmen for every part of gun manufacture from stock making to barrel turning, epitomised what a 17th Century visitor called "the skill, adaptability and energy of the inhabitants."

Birmingham's metalworking skills became a focal point of industrial development, for while the ideas may have been invented elsewhere, turning them into reality had to be entrusted to the practical men of iron.

Nothing illustrated this better than the development of steam power.

For not only was there a good market among the many mines and forges of Birmingham and South Staffordshire for the new technology of the Industrial Revolution, but also a ready supply of financial backers and engineers ready to turn theory into practice.

Thomas Newcomen of Dartmouth sold his first 'fire engine,' with the financial backing of a Bromsgrove merchant, to pump water from a mine in Tipton in 1712.

Newcomen's engine was crude and inefficient, and it was the Scot, James Watt, who made Newcomen's engine cheaper to run and so widen the market away from the coalfields where fuel was cheap.

James Watt travelled south to Birmingham to try to get his ideas onto the market, and there he joined up with Matthew Boulton.

Boulton was a toymaker, producing steel belt buckles and other objects, but he was by no means the largest manufacturer and trader in Birmingham at the start of the Industrial Revolution.

That honour went to the buttonmaker John Taylor who is credited with developing specialisation, with workers performing one task each in the process of producing buttons or enamelled snuff boxes.

Taylor employed some 500 people in 1766 when his new processes were described by Lord and Lady Shelburne.

Another major employer was John Baskerville, famous for inventing the printing type named after him, who originally developed and marketed the Japanning process, applying black lacquer to bare metal goods to produce an attractive finish.

His factory was near the present day Baskerville House, close by the International Convention Centre. ▷

TOP LEFT. PROOF HOUSE, 1813.
ABOVE. TRIBUTE TO A PIONEER — BASKERVILLE HOUSE CELEBRATES THE INVENTOR OF THE TYPEFACE, JOHN BASKERVILLE.
RIGHT. MAN OF LETTERS, — JOHN BASKERVILLE AND HIS TYPEFACE.
BOTTOM LEFT. A TRADE SURVIVES — GUNMAKING, 1989.

Matthew Boulton sprang to fame because of his Soho Manufactory, a series of purpose-built workshops set up in 1764 at the bottom of the garden of what Lady Shelburne called "his pretty little house about one mile out of town."

A mill already existed on the site, powered by the Handsworth Brook, and it was on the turnpike road to Wednesbury, giving access to the South Staffordshire ironworks and coalmines in the Black Country.

It would not be long before the Manufactory was served by the new canal, in which Boulton had a share, so cutting the costs of transport.

Birmingham eventually stood at the centre of the 'Silver Cross' of the canal system, the new waterways dramatically cut costs and helped industry to thrive.

Soho employed more than a thousand, but was not a factory in the modern sense, more a collection of workshops with teams of craftsmen making different products, grouped around central services.

A similar concept exists today in nearby Hockley Port, where enterprise workshops help new businesses to find their feet.

But Soho was operated under an overall Master, Boulton, who gave the enterprise a common philosophy, and endeavoured to give Soho products a high reputation.

Boulton was behind the establishment of the Birmingham Assay Office in 1773.

Working conditions were good for the period, and Boulton introduced a social insurance scheme in 1792.

He was also aware of the progress of the world about him, always looking for new ideas, and so attracted James Watt.

The two first met in 1768 when a steam engine was used to recycle water from the tailrace of Boulton's mill to the millpond.

They went into partnership in 1774 and an early Boulton and Watt engine was installed to pump water on the Birmingham Canal in 1777.

The engine is now in the Birmingham Museum of Science and Industry, in Newhall Street, which was itself the site of a technological advance.

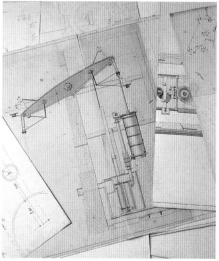

The museum inherited the site of Elkington, Mason & Co., who patented electroplating in 1840 and gave birth to a trade which is still carried on in Hockley.

But Boulton and Watt's great leap forward was the invention of the rotative engine, which turned shafts to operate machinery, and they set up the Soho Foundry in 1796 to make the new engines.

The site in Foundry Road is still occupied, by the Avery scale works, and is all that remains of the partners' enterprise, for the original Manufactory was demolished in 1863.

Science and philosophy came together through Boulton, Watt, Baskerville and others such as Joseph Priestley, the discoverer of oxygen, the naturalist Erasmus Darwin, Dr. William Withering who discovered the use of digitalis as a heart stimulant, and the potter Josiah Wedgwood.

TOP LEFT. FIRST OF MANY — THE SOHO MANUFACTORY, 1764. RIGHT. DESIGNS ON THE MARKETPLACE — FROM BOULTON'S NOTEBOOKS. LEFT. CHEMICAL PIONEER AND LUNAR LUMINARY — DR. JOSEPH PRIESTLEY, DISCOVERER OF OXYGEN.

From 1766 these and others gathered for monthly discussions, travelling by the light of the moon, and calling themselves the Lunar Society.

The danger of their nocturnal travels must have been enough encouragement for the Scot, William Murdoch, who had joined Boulton and Watt, to pursue his ideas for artificial light.

Murdoch was another steam engineer, who demonstrated a model steam road locomotive in 1784 which was ahead of its time.

Murdoch's coal gas first lit the Soho Manufactory in 1802 and by 1805 the gas production plant was a major product.

Soho had one more bequest to modern Birmingham, for it also contained a major mint, with coining presses of Soho design and manufacture.

The presses were key items in the auction of the Manufactory in 1850 and were by that time the only major mint outside the Royal Mint in London.

They were bought by Ralph Heaton II, a Birmingham diesinker who bought the

associated blanking machinery and set up the Birmingham Mint.

Today the mint, which moved to Icknield Street, Hockley in 1860, is one of only two private mints in Britain and both are in Birmingham.

The other is at Witton, owned by IMI.

The growth of industry demanded finance and John Taylor the buttonmaker joined the ironmonger Sampson Lloyd II in 1765 to set up Taylors and Lloyds Bank in Dale End, the foundation of the modern Lloyds Bank.

The Midland Bank also has its roots in Birmingham, founded as the Birmingham & Midland in 1836, in the same year as a constituent of Barclay's Bank, the Birmingham Town and District Banking Company.

The Bank of England set up a branch in 1827 which quickly surpassed the local banks for supplying paper money, and today is second only to London in the amount of money it issues.

The early 19th Century also saw the Chamber of Commerce born in 1813, formed out of the Birmingham Commercial Committee of 1783.

The Birmingham Stock Exchange was founded in 1845 to regulate share dealings

among the city's growing band of stockbrokers in the midst of the Railway Mania, the boom period for new railway schemes which when constructed put Birmingham at the centre of an Iron Cross and cutting costs, just like the canals before them.

It was a time of widening share ownership, and the Birmingham Exchange of today still pursues the theme.

Now amalgamated into the Midlands and Western Unit of The International Stock Exchange, it is the only trading floor left in England, after the closure of the London equity floor in 1987. ▷

TOP LEFT. TRIBUTE IN BRONZE — BOULTON, MURDOCH AND WATT, PIONEERS OF THE INDUSTRIAL REVOLUTION.

ABOVE. THE BANK OF ENGLAND SET UP ITS BIRMINGHAM BRANCH IN 1827 — AND THERE HAS BEEN A STOCK EXCHANGE SINCE 1845.

LEFT. THE BIRMINGHAM MINT.

Birmingham has also re-emerged as a major financial centre in the 1980s, as the demands for capital have again increased.

Its chartered accountants form the largest branch of the English Institute of Chartered Accountants outside London, and it is an important centre of commercial law.

Its importance is such that leading Japanese banks have established branches, and the leading merchant banks are also represented.

Their presence is helping to re-establish local ownership, after a period when many famous companies were taken over to have their identities submerged, and their head offices moved away.

Those still governed from Birmingham include Lucas Industries, founded by Joseph Lucas in 1876 to make lamps, and Cadbury Schweppes, which began in 1824 as a grocer and tea dealer.

Lucas expanded first in the bicycle boom of the 1880s, then with the motor industry after pioneers like F.W. Lanchester and Herbert Austin.

Lucas supplied components, one among many Birmingham firms to serve the new technology of the 20th Century, especially after Austin set up his works at Longbridge in 1905.

Austin's factory pioneered popular motoring with the Austin 7, followed many years later in 1959 with the revolutionary Mini, which like other Longbridge products still uses Lucas components.

Lucas has also developed control and engine management systems for the aerospace industry and its engineers worked closely with Sir Frank Whittle to develop jet engines in the 1940s.

Cadbury Schweppes is the product of a Quaker family, and in 1879 moved to the green fields of Bournville to set up a model factory and housing which pioneered town planning and garden city concepts.

Like Quaker families elsewhere, it has endowed many local charities and remains a powerful force in modern Birmingham.

Gun manufacture reached its zenith after the foundation of the Birmingham Small Arms Company in 1861, later to become a wide-ranging conglomerate from machine tools to motor cycles, but it has dwindled to a handful of firms, though the traditional division of skills remains.

The jewellery industry which developed from the 'toy' trade remains firmly established in what was originally the Colmore Estate.

Indeed, the area has found new life as the City Council has developed the Jewellery Quarter as a conservation area.

The recession of the 1980s caused many companies to cut back and even to close down, and the city has had to try to attract new business to replace them.

Birmingham has not traditionally been considered as a natural centre for service industry.

Yet the initiative of Birmingham Chamber of Industry and Commerce and Birmingham City Council which in 1976 led to the opening of the purpose-built National Exhibition Centre spurred a boom in service sector jobs.

The centre now houses most of the major European industrial exhibitions, and is an important entertainment venue.

The development of the International Convention Centre close to the heart of the city will reinforce the position.

The impetus is fuelled by the city's position at the centre of the Victorian-built rail network, and the late 20th Century Motorway system, as well as an international airport close by the NEC.

The airport is also home to Britain's only inland freeport, where goods can be imported, processed and exported free of customs tariffs.

Birmingham had scant recognition as a centre for the new electronics-based industries, despite the long association of Lucas, GEC and other electrical companies, as well as the expertise of its universities.

The position is changing and the locally-founded Apricot Computers has established its research and development centre on the

campus of Birmingham University.

The city's main thrust to develop and attract new technology is through the Aston Science Park, a joint venture with Aston University and Lloyds Bank.

It has set out to redevelop 22 acres of former industrial land occupied by semi-derelict factories, bringing in new science-based industry which can link directly with

Aston University and act as a forcing-house for new industry.

An uncompromising marketing platform, looking for high quality occupants meant that it took almost three years before tenancies and job creation began to take off.

By 1988 there were 50 companies on site, with 500 jobs, with the prospect of 1,500 to 2,000 jobs by 1994, in a hundred companies.

Further development of the science park concept is expected in the Birmingham Heartlands area, Britain's first privately-backed urban development corporation.

The inclusion of Birmingham and the West Midlands in the Government Assisted Area framework from 1984 has helped to produce money to attract industry and counter the better financial attractions of Scotland and Wales.

It has also helped to attract funds from the European Economic Community which are in the main used to improve the infrastructure and promote job training.

The City Council has also taken a lead in attracting industry through a package which has drawn admiration from industry and commerce.

The package has many financial incentives, but still relies heavily on the nature of the city's location and its access to markets and to a variety of skills.

Where else could today's entrepreneur feel so much at home, but Birmingham. ◇ ◇

TOP. INTERNATIONAL GATEWAY — BIRMINGHAM INTERNATIONAL AIRPORT WITH ITS PIONEERING MAGLEV LINK TO THE STATION AND NEC: ITS CARS FLOAT ON MAGNETIC FORCE.

CENTRE. INNER-CITY REVIVAL — ASTON SCIENCE PARK, SEEDBED FOR NEW SCIENCE-BASED INDUSTRY, A SECOND INDUSTRIAL REVOLUTION.

LEFT. ELECTRONIC FUTURE — APRICOT GROWS AT BIRMINGHAM.

The stranger lurked in the doorway of the empty house. Waiting.

The night of January 12, 1987 was one of the coldest in living memory.

Jerry Hibbert of East Sheen had been working late in his animation studio and it was 10.30 before he got home.

The sight that greeted him when he arrived was enough to make anyone animated. A mains pipe in the attic had burst and water had been cascading through his house since lunchtime.

The Artist's impression.

Icicles five feet long hung from the roof; the walls were coated in sheets of ice.

But if it was Antarctica outside, it was Atlantis inside.

Water poured down the walls and streamed from the ceiling. Pictures and lamps had been swept aside; furniture and carpets were soaked.

And the dining-room ceiling was now on the dining-room floor.

By the time an emergency plumber had come and turned off the mains, Jerry Hibbert had had enough. He locked up his sodden home and went to stay with friends.

But while he was settling between the sheets, his house was settling under a blanket.

Of snow. So much snow that by morning East Sheen had ground to a halt.

Undeterred, Jerry Hibbert began phoning round for help with the mopping up.

He called the electrician, the plumber and the cleaners. But in view of the weather none of them could promise a prompt arrival.

Then he called his insurance advisor.

He put Mr. Hibbert in touch with the local Commercial Union branch. They said they would send someone round to his house as soon as possible.

After bidding his friends and their nice warm house a fond farewell, Mr. Hibbert set out on the cold journey home.

He wasn't the first to arrive.

Waiting in the doorway was a stranger. The man from Commercial Union.

After introducing himself our man set to work. He inspected the damage.

He checked that Mr. Hibbert had somewhere to stay until his house was fit to live in once again.

And he made sure there were people organised to carry out repairs.

But repairs cost money.

So he also authorised Mr. Hibbert to spend up to £1,000 on covering the cost, which we confirmed in a letter two days later.

The work of our local office didn't finish there however. Mr. Hibbert had been in the process of selling his house when the disaster struck.

Now he wanted the claim transferred to the new owner.

We immediately agreed to organise the transaction, so that the deal could be completed as swiftly as possible.

Because at Commercial Union we don't like to keep our clients waiting. Ever.

We won't make a drama out of a crisis.

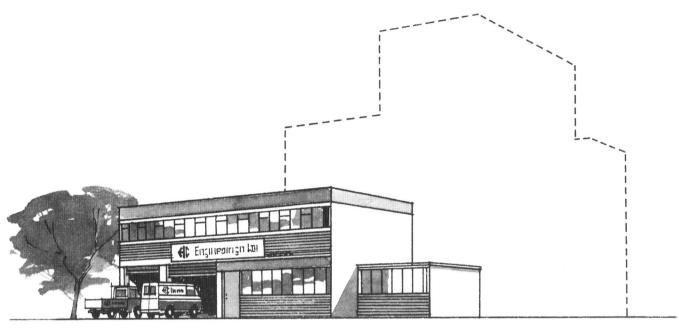

Helping businesses grow is a growing part of our business.

The Price Waterhouse Independent Business Group has extensive experience in helping to overcome the problems of firms wanting to grow. And it is this kind of experience that can make all the difference between success and failure.

For example raising money, managing growth and planning for the future in the most effective manner, are just some of the areas where the right advice is crucial.

If you are worried about the problems of business growth or need advice on starting a business or developing a business plan we can almost certainly help you.

Why not call George Carter on (021) 200 3000. Surely it's worth a phone call.

GAS. FUELLING BIRMINGHAM'S SUCCESS FOR OVER A CENTURY.

It was one of Birmingham's founding fathers, Matthew Boulton, who first used gas in the City. That was in 1802, in his factory in Handsworth.

Then, Birmingham was just another town. Now it is one of the great Cities of the world.

We're proud to say we've played our part in fuelling Birmingham's growth. A part which we're looking forward to continuing in the future.

Because Birmingham is built on successful commerce and industry. And we have the energy to help all kinds of business – big and small. Talk to the experts now on 021-711 2293. You'll be in good company.

British Gas
West Midlands
ENERGY IS OUR BUSINESS

THE BIRMINGHAM CENTENARY FESTIVAL CALENDAR OF EVENTS

The Birmingham Centenary Festival is a celebration of every aspect of this great City's life and will go on throughout the year, a 365 day party. A birthday party is about enjoyment and Centenary Year in Birmingham will have fun in plenty.

The worlds of the arts, sport, science, education, industry, commerce and entertainment will feature in over 600 events of astonishing variety, celebrating Birmingham's past, present and future.

And there's more to come, for this calendar represents only those events confirmed before November 1988. Such has been the response to the Centenary that new events continue to pour in. Details of these will be announced in the City Council's "Whole Lot of City Going On" magazines and in the local press over the next twelve months.

Many of the events in the programme have been suggested and are being organised by the people of Birmingham themselves. Many are being specially staged in Birmingham to honour the City's 100th birthday.

"They possessed a vivacity...their very step along the street showed alacrity... Hospitality seemed to claim this happy people for her own."

WILLIAM HUTTON, HISTORIAN, 1841
about the people of Birmingham

Many are established events from Birmingham's exciting annual calendar. Many are events being brought to the City for the first time and will make Birmingham their permanent home.

The Centenary Festival represents the most comprehensive programme of events, exhibitions and attractions ever staged in a British City. Birmingham will blazon its pride abroad. It will invite the world, the Nation and its neighbours to share its sense of accomplishment.

No wonder there's a big smile on the face of Birmingham today, it is a time of celebration — Welcome to Birmingham's Centenary Festival!

For further information about the Birmingham Centenary Festival contact Peter Mearns, Centenary Director, Birmingham City Council, Council House, Birmingham B1 1BB, England. Telephone 021-235 2208

Booking Information — Birmingham Convention and Visitor Bureau, Ticket Shop and Tourist Information Centre, Telephone 021-643 2514

Access for the Disabled — you are advised to check in advance with the venue concerned.

Every endeavour has been made to ensure that the information contained in this programme is correct at the time of going to press. The Publisher cannot accept any responsibility for any errors contained in the programme or for any amendment made to the information.

January
Diary of events from 1st – 26th January

VIP RECORD FAIR
Library Exhibition Hall
1st Jan, 11th Mar, 8th Apr, 6th May,
3rd June, 12th Aug, 4th Nov, 2nd Dec
Admission £1.25
(75p after 11.00 am)
Details: Birmingham City Council
021-235 3392

BIRMINGHAM CITY v OLDHAM ATHLETIC
St. Andrews Ground
2nd January
Details: Birmingham City F.C. plc
021-772 0101

RUGBY – MOSELEY v GLOUCESTER
The Reddings
2nd January
Details: Moseley Football Club
021-449 2149

PLAY "TOAD OF TOAD HALL"
Highbury Little Theatre
3rd-7th January
Details: Highbury Community Theatre
Arts Centre 021-373 1961

ARIOSO QUARTET SERIES
Birmingham & Midland Institute
5th January
"Virtuoso Bass" Tom Martin with Joyce
Woodhead (Piano) and Margaret Field
(Soprano)
Details: The Birmingham and
Midland Institute 021-236 3591

RETIREMENT – PLANNING FOR A NEW LIFE EXHIBITION
NEC
5th-8th January
Details: National Exhibition Centre
021-780 4171

THE HOLIDAY AND TRAVEL FAIR
NEC
5th-8th January
Britain's biggest international public
holiday show will be officially opened by
the reigning Miss Great Britain.
Details: National Exhibition Centre
021-780 4171

BRITISH CYCLO-CROSS CHAMPIONSHIPS
Sutton Park
7th January
Details: Birmingham City Council
021-235 3008

"MESSIAH" WITH PERIOD INSTRUMENTS – EX CATHEDRA
Birmingham Cathedral
7th January
Sponsored by Colliers Jaguar
Details: Ex Cathedra 021-235 2208

BIRMINGHAM NETBALL LEAGUE – BIRMINGHAM COUNTY v KENT
Great Barr School
7th January
Details Birmingham Netball League
021-458 2000 Ex 3417

RUGBY – MOSELEY v WEST HARTLEPOOL
The Reddings
7th January
Details: Moseley Football Club
021-449 2149

WORCESTER INDOOR TOURNAMENT – HOCKEY
Cocks Moors Woods Leisure Centre
7th & 8th January
Details: Midland Counties Hockey
Association 0564 779101

PINSENT CELEBRITY CONCERT
Adrian Boult Hall
10th January
Malcolm Messiter, Oboe. Tina
Gruenberg, Violin. Yuko Inoue, Viola.
Lowri Blake, Cello.
Details: Birmingham School of Music
021-331 5908

CBSO TUESDAY SERIES
Birmingham Town Hall
10th January
Brahms (orch Schoenberg) Piano
Quartet in G Minor, Janacek; Glagolitic
Mass. Conductor Simon Rattle.
Details: CBSO 021-236 1555

"SLEEPING BEAUTY"
Victoria Public House,
John Bright Street
10th-15th January
Details: The Young Pretenders
021-236 3333 x2259

CBSO WEDNESDAY SERIES
Birmingham Town Hall
11th January
Brahms – Piano Quartet in G Minor,
Janacek – Glagolitic Mass. Conductor
Simon Rattle
Details: CBSO 021-236 1555

PRE-RAPHAELITE EXHIBITIONS
Museum and Art Gallery

HOLY GRAIL TAPESTRIES – BURNE-JONES
12th January – 2nd April
The first opportunity for several years to
see the series of tapestries illustrating the
Legend of the Holy Grail. Designed by
Edward Burne-Jones and woven by Morris
& Co., these represent an extraordinary
achievement in the art of weaving.

WILLIAM MORRIS – PATTERN DESIGNER
12th January – 30th April
To accompany the exhibition of
tapestries, a selection of original William
Morris drawings for wallpapers and
fabrics will be on show.

PRE-RAPHAELITE DRAWINGS
12th January – 30th April
More than 200 drawings by Ford Madox
Brown, Dante Gabriel Rossetti, John
Millais, Frederick Sandys, Holman Hunt,
Edward Burne-Jones and others make up
this exhibition, drawn entirely from
Birmingham's important but rarely seen
collection of 19th century drawings.
The City's outstanding Pre-Raphaelite
paintings will, as usual, be on show
together with a selection of Birmingham's
unrivalled collection of paintings and
monumental watercolours by Sir
Edward Burne-Jones, probably the City's
most famous artist and one of the most
influential figures in the Victorian art
world.
Details: Birmingham City Council
021-235 2800

VISIT BY QUEEN VICTORIA AND CHARTER DAY CELEBRATIONS

VISIT BY QUEEN VICTORIA

City Centre
13th January
6pm onwards

"It is with very considerable pleasure and pride that the Mayor, Burgesses and Townspeople are honoured by the visit of Victoria, by the grace of God, of the United Kingdom of Great Britain and Ireland, Queen, Defender of the Faith, Empress of India, together with her son, His Royal Highness, Edward, the Prince of Wales on the occasion, and for the purpose of conferring by Royal Charter upon the Borough of Birmingham the title of City." 100 years ago the Borough of Birmingham became a City.

While crowds gather in excitement and anticipation in Chamberlain Square a steam engine pulls ceremoniously into Snowhill Station... The people lining the platform cheer and wave flags as Her Majesty Queen Victoria and her son, His Royal Highness Edward Prince of Wales, step from the train to be greeted by local dignitaries.

Imagine the accompanying splendour, as the Mounted Band of H.M. Life Guards leads a procession of the royal retinue in state coaches along the length of Colmore Row and into Victoria Square, to unveil a commemorative statue of the Queen in honour of the grand occasion.

And The City celebrates! A glorious feast of Victorian entertainments and sideshows, a musical concert and spectacular firework display.

Watch history magically come to life. Join the new citizens in this 'cast-of-thousands,' authentic enactment of the royal visit to launch our year-long Centenary Festival. Central Television will be filming the festivities so dress in Victorian costume and be among the cheering throng. Celebrate Birmingham's 100th Birthday as a City!

Details: Birmingham City Council
021-235 2208

CHARTER DAY

City Centre
14th January

Today is the 100th Birthday of our City and we're having a party to remember! There'll be lots of free entertainment throughout the City Centre with music on every corner, dancing in the streets and festival fun for all!

The weather can't dampen our spirits or hamper our revelry... So be there!... Join in... It's the biggest Birthday bonanza ever!

PRIDE OF PLACE EXHIBITION

Central Library
13th January — 10th February
A prestigious exhibition to celebrate Birmingham's Centenary Year.
It will provide a focus for the City's social and industrial past as well as an opportunity to promote current and future business activity.
Exhibitors will be encouraged to enter into the spirit of a Century of Celebration by displaying archive material, as well as exhibiting the products and services of 1989 and the next 100 years.
The exhibition will be open to the public from 10.00am until 6.00pm (closed Sunday). There will be a special late opening on Friday 13th January until 9.00pm, as part of the official festivities taking place in the City Centre.
Details: Birmingham City Council 021-235 3392

QUANTRO SOUNDS – MUSIC IN THE OPEN AIR

City Centre
13th-15th January
Details: Quantroitone Sound Systems 021-551 0343

ASTON VILLA F.C. v NEWCASTLE UNITED

Villa Park
14th January
Details: Aston Villa Football Club Ltd 021-328 1722

QUIZ GAME

Community Meeting Place, Tugford Road
14th January
Details: Middle Park Residents Association 021-476 1210

CENTENARY PEAL BY THE BELLS OF THE CATHEDRAL

Birmingham Cathedral
14th January
Details: The Provost, Birmingham Cathedral 021-236 6323

CENTENARY FESTIVAL SERVICE

Birmingham Cathedral
14th January
A Festival Service at the Cathedral with the Archbishop of Canterbury, preceded by a civic procession from the Council House to St. Philip's. An Anthem specially written to commemorate the Centenary will be sung by the Cathedral Choir.
Details: The Provost, Birmingham Cathedral 021-236 6323

CENTENARY CONCERT BY THE BIRMINGHAM SINFONIETTA

Birmingham Cathedral
14th January
Details: The Provost, Birmingham Cathedral 021-236 6323

BIRMINGHAM MIDSHIRES INTERNATIONAL INDOOR TOURNAMENT – HOCKEY

Cocks Moors Woods Leisure Centre
14th-15th January
Details: Midlands Counties Hockey Association 0564 779101

EUROPEAN ICE FIGURE SKATING CHAMPIONSHIPS

NEC
17th-22nd January
Sponsored by SkateElectric
Europe's top skaters will be in action at the NEC when the European Figure Skating Championships return to Britain after an absence of 50 years. The spectacular opening Gala celebrates the City of Birmingham's 100th Birthday and 100 years of ice-skating with more than 100 skaters taking part. The Gala of Champions will take place in the presence of The Princess Royal, HRH Princess Anne.
The provisional timetable:
Tuesday 17th January
Arena 13.30
Dance — Compulsory Dances
Arena 19.00
Opening Ceremony
Arena 20.00
Pairs: Original Programme
Wednesday 18th January
Arena 14.30
Men: Original Programme
Arena 19.30
Pairs: Free Skating
Thursday 19th January
Forum 10.30
Ladies Compulsory Figures
Arena 14.30
Dance: OSPD
Arena 18.30
Men: Free Skating
Friday 20th January
Arena 14.00
Ladies: Original Programme
Arena 18.30
Dance: Free Dance
Saturday 21st January
Arena 13.15
Ladies: Free Skating
Sunday 22nd January
Arena 14.00
Gala of Champions
Details: National Skating Association 01-253 0910

THE RAPHAEL ENSEMBLE – R.C.M.C.

Midlands Arts Centre
18th January
Details: Midlands Arts Centre 021-440 4221

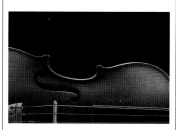

BSM LUNCHTIME CONCERT

Recital Hall
18th January
Malcolm Wilson Piano
Details: Birmingham School of Music 021-331 5908

ARIOSO QUARTET SERIES

Birmingham & Midland Institute
19th January
Schubert: Quartettsatz, Brahms: Clarinet Quintet with Colin Parr (Clarinet)
Details: The Birmingham and Midland Institute 021-236 3591

CBSO THURSDAY SERIES

Birmingham Town Hall
19th January
Jonathan Lloyd — Symphony No 1 (Premiere), Mozart — Piano Concerto in B flat (K595), Haydn — Symphony No 90 in C. Conductor Simon Rattle. Soloist Imogen Cooper
Details: CBSO 021-236 1555

WOMEN IN COMMERCE & INDUSTRY IN 19th CENTURY BIRMINGHAM

Gilligans, Moseley Road
19th January
Lecture
Details: Birmingham Association of Women 021-444 2119

ORCHESTRA DA CAMERA – DAVID PONSFORD

Adrian Boult Hall
20th January
Details: Birmingham School of Music 021-331 5908

RUGBY – MOSELEY v NORTHAMPTON
The Reddings
20th January
Details: Moseley Football Club
021-449 2149

BIRMINGHAM CITY v WATFORD
St Andrews Ground
21st January
Details: Birmingham City F.C. plc
021-772 0101

BIRMINGHAM SCHOOLS' CONCERT ORCHESTRA
Adrian Boult Hall
21st January
Combination of classical, film and show music
Details: Birmingham Schools' Concert Orchestra 021-440 4111

"PAINT THE CITY" EXHIBITION
RBSA Gallery
21st January – 11th February
60 invited artists show paintings of Birmingham
Details: Royal Birmingham Society of Artists

BIRMINGHAM/WEST MIDLANDS WEDDING & FIRST HOME EXHIBITION.
NEC
21st-22nd January
Details: GHC Exhibitions 041-332 6776

THE FINE ARTS BRASS ENSEMBLE
Midlands Arts Centre
22nd January
Details: Midlands Arts Centre
021-440 4221

BSM CHAMBER ORCHESTRA
Sutton Coldfield Town Hall
23rd January
Kenneth Sillitoe , Handel , Bach, Rossini, Tchaikovsky
Details: Birmingham School of Music
021-331 5902

CBSO TUESDAY SERIES
Birmingham Town Hall
24th January
Debussy — Incidental Music to King Lear, Rachmaninov — Piano Concerto No 2, Franz Schmit — Symphony No 4. Conductor Simon Rattle.
Soloist John Lill
Details: CBSO 021-236 1555

BSM CHAMBER ORCHESTRA
Adrian Boult Hall
24th January
Kenneth Sillitoe, Handel, Bach, Rossini, Tchaikovsky
Details: Birmingham School of Music
021-331 5908

BSM LUNCHTIME CONCERT
Recital Hall
25th January
Richard Weigall, Oboe.
Frank Wibaut, Piano
Details: Birmingham School of Music
021-331 5908

NATIONAL CONFERENCE – GEESE THEATRE CO.
Midlands Arts Centre
25th January
Details: Geese Theatre Company
021-551 5116

LUNCHTIME CENTENARY ORGAN RECITAL – THOMAS TROTTER
Birmingham Town Hall
25th January
A special recital to celebrate the City's Centenary by the City Organist, the internationally renowned Thomas Trotter
Details: Birmingham City Council
021-236 2392

LUNCHTIME CONCERT SEASON – MCPMS
Birmingham Cathedral
27th January
Songs from Vienna. Famous Excerpts from the Operettas of Lehar and Strauss.
Mozart — Duet from "Don Giovanni"
Strauss — Viennese Waltzes.
Details: The Midlands Chamber Players Music Society 021-449 2352

RUGBY – PILKINGTON CUP
The Reddings
28th January
Details: Moseley Football Club
021-449 2149

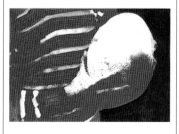

INTER-AREA RIFLE SHOOTING FINALS – 14-Under 21
Four Dwellings Forum
28th January
Details: Birmingham City Council
021-440 6841

BINGHAM QUARTET & RAPHAEL WALLFISCH
Adrian Boult Hall
28th January
Mendelssohn Quartet op. 44/1 in D, Shostakovitch No 1 Op. 49 in C. Schubert Quintet Op.163 D956 in C
Details: Birmingham Chamber Music Society 021-643 7041

"MURDERER" BY ANTHONY SHAFFER
The Crescent Theatre
28th January – 11th February
Details: The Crescent Theatre
021-420 5007

LADA BRITISH CITIES INDOOR TOURNAMENT – HOCKEY
Aston Villa Leisure Centre
28th-29th January
Details: Midlands Counties Hockey Association 0564 779101

CENTENARY FINANCIAL QUIZ – CLOSING DATE
29th January
Entry form obtainable from Council House reception and Libraries
Details: Birmingham City Council
021-235 3107

ST PAUL'S DAY FESTIVAL
St Paul's Church
29th January
Preacher Rt. Revd. Mark Santer, Bishop of Birmingham
Details: St. Paul's Church, Birmingham
021-427 5141

BSM LUNCHTIME CONCERT
Recital Hall
31st January
Elise Ross — Soprano, Malcom Wilson — Piano
Details: Birmingham School of Music
021-331 5908

MIDLAND MUSIC MAKERS GRAND OPERA SOCIETY CONCERT
George Cadbury Hall
January
Details: Midlands Music Makers Grand Opera Society 021-308 4093

BEGINNERS COURSES IN JU-JITSU & KICK BOXING
Bushido Ju-Jitsu Centre
January – October
Details: Bushido Ju-Jitsu Centre
021-300 6688

CHILDREN'S CHRISTMAS ART COMPETITION
Central Library
January
Sponsored by Sandvik
Details: Birmingham City Council
021-235 3392

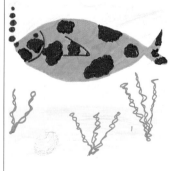

February
Diary of events from 2nd — 28th February

JUNIOR CHAMBER CHARITY DEBATING COMPETITION
January — March
Debating competition involving companies and organisations in the city with proceeds going to charity.
Details: Junior Chamber Birmingham 021-454 6171

POSTER COMPETITION WITH DAILY NEWS
January
Details: Birmingham City Council 021-454 6001

"JACK AND THE BEANSTALK"
Birmingham Hippodrome
January — February
Starring Russ Abbot
Details: Birmingham Hippodrome 021-622 7486

"THE WOMAN IN BLACK"
Birmingham Repertory Theatre — Studio
January
A chilling ghost story for a winter night
Details: Birmingham Repertory Theatre 021-236 4455

"ALICE IN WONDERLAND"
Birmingham Repertory Theatre
January
Details: Birmingham Repertory Theatre 021-236 4455

CBSO THURSDAY SERIES
Birmingham Town Hall
2nd February
Britten — Sinfonia da Requiem, Schubert — Symphony No 9 (The Great).
Conductor Simon Rattle
Details: CBSO 021-236 1555

ARIOSO QUARTET SERIES
Birmingham & Midland Institute
2nd February
John Ireland Sonata No 1, Beethoven "Kreutzer" Sonata, Jeremy Ballard (Violin), Margaret Newman (Piano)
Details: The Birmingham & Midland Institutè 021-236 3591

A VICTORIAN HIRING FAIR
Colmers Farm School
2nd-3rd February
Details: Colmers Farm (Senior School) 021-453 1778

ASTON VILLA F.C. v SHEFFIELD WEDNESDAY
Villa Park
4th February
Details: Aston Villa Football Club Ltd 021-328 1722

RUGBY — MOSELEY v RICHMOND
The Reddings
4th February
Details: Moseley Football Club 021-449 2149

OPEN DAY AND CENTENARY CELEBRATION
Stone Hall Adult Education Centre
4th February
Details: Birmingham City Council Department 021-784 0888

CONCERT IN AID OF THE NSPCC
Birmingham Town Hall
4th February
Conductor Simon Rattle, Soloist John Lill — Debussy, Rachmaninov and Schubert
Details: CBSO 021-236 1555

THE SERIES
Adrian Boult Hall
4th February
An exciting collaboration between the Birmingham Contemporary Music Group, Birmingham Jazz and the Arts Council's Contemporary Music Network brings the work of Jack De Johnette and John Surman to Birmingham as the sixth in a series of 10 concerts.
Details: Birmingham Jazz 021-414 5703

BACH IN LEIPZIG
Birmingham Cathedral
4th February
Cantatas 161 and 182. Motet 'Jesu meine Freude.' Harpsichord Concerto in D minor.
Details: Halcyon Ensemble 021-476 2800

CBSO ADOPT-A-PLAYER
Central Library
4th-10th February
The CBSO's 'Adopt-a-Player Scheme' sponsored by McDonald's, helps to break down the barriers between children and professional musicians by involving the players in the children's creative composition work in the classroom. This is based on a piece which they hear in a CBSO rehearsal and concert.
The exhibition in the Central Library features a display of the children's creative work inspired by Debussy's Images.
Details: Birmingham City Council 021-235 3392

WHO'S AFRAID OF VIRGINIA WOOLF?
Birmingham Repertory Theatre
4th-25th February
Details: The Birmingham Repertory Theatre 021-236 4455

CHINESE NEW YEAR CELEBRATIONS
5th February
6th February sees the beginning of the Chinese Year of the Snake. Birmingham's Chinese community will be celebrating the occasion on the 5th February.
Details: Birmingham Chinese Community Centre 021-622 3003

INTER-AREA TABLE TENNIS FINALS
John Willmott School/Leisure Centre
6th & 8th February
Details: Birmingham City Council 021-440 6841

BOOK WEEK
St Benedict's Infant School
6th-8th February
Details: St Benedict's Infant School 021-772 0087

PANCAKE RACE — SHROVE TUESDAY
Flea Market
7th February
Details: Birmingham City Council 021-622 3452

SCHOOL OF ARCHITECTURE EXHIBITION
Central Library
7th February — 2nd March
Details: Birmingham City Council 021-235 3392

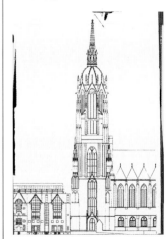

EXHIBITION –
"MY IMAGE OF OLD INDIA" by
MR MOHAN MISTRY
Central Library
7th February — 5th March
Details: Birmingham City Council
021-235 3392

PLAY "ALL MY SONS" –
ARTHUR MILLER
Highbury Little Theatre
7th-18th February
Details: Highbury Theatre Arts Centre
021-373 1961

CBSO WEDNESDAY SERIES
Birmimgham Town Hall
8th February
Boulez — Eclat, Bartok — Voilin Concerto
No 2, Debussy — Images. Conductor
Simon Rattle. Soloist Kyung-Wha Chung
Details: CBSO 021-236 1555

MIDLANDS YOUTH JAZZ
ORCHESTRA
Midlands Arts Centre
8th February
Details: Midlands Arts Centre
021-440 4221

CBSO THURSDAY SERIES
Birmingham Town Hall
9th February
Boulez: Eclat, Bartok: Violin Concerto
No 2, Debussy: Images
Conductor Simon Rattle.
Soloist Kyung-Wha Chung.
Details: CBSO 021-236 1555

AMBACH CHAMBER ORCHESTRA
Adrian Boult Hall
10th February
"Sweet 17" Early Mozart.
Details: Grosvenor Concerts
021-331 5908

MAGIC FLUTE
11th February
Details: City of Birmingham Touring
Opera 021-440 5832

CBSO BENEVOLENT FUND CONCERT
Birmingham Town Hall
11th February
Conductor Simon Rattle, Soloist Kyung
Wha Chung
Details: CBSO 021-236 1555

BIRMINGHAM TRAMPOLINE
CHAMPIONSHIPS
Birmingham Sports Centre
11th February
Details: British Trampoline Federation
021-552 6272

"THE JAIL BREAK"
Throughout Birmingham
11th February
A sponsored event for young people to
travel by public transport to all corners of
the City in a challenge of wits and bus-
chasing style
Details: Birmingham City Council
021-440 6841

BIRMINGHAM CITY v
A.F.C. BOURNEMOUTH
St. Andrews Ground
11th February
Details: Birmingham City F.C. plc.
021-772 0101

CIRCA 1500 –
EARLY MUSIC NETWORK
Midlands Arts Centre
12th February
Details: Midlands Arts Centre 021-440
4221

DIVISIONAL SCHOOLS
QUADRANGULAR HOCKEY
TOURNAMENT
Fox Hollies Leisure Centre
12th February
Details: Midland Counties Hockey
Association 0564 779101

"IN THE DAYS OF QUEEN VICTORIA"
Jonathan's Restaurant
13th-19th February
Including Victorian Valentine evening
and Sherlock Holmes evening.
Culminating in a Victorian Banquet on
the 19th February.
Details: Jonathan's 021-429 3757

PINSENT CELEBRITY CONCERT
Adrian Boult Hall
14th February
Frank Lloyd, Horn. Kenneth Essex, Viola.
Delme String Quartet
Details: Birmingham School of Music
021-331 5908

CBSO TUESDAY SERIES
Birmingham Town Hall
14th February
Michael Torke — Vanada, Debussy — Jeux,
Elgar — Violin Concerto. Conductor
Simon Rattle. Soloist Oscar Shumsky
Details: CBSO 021-236 1555

WOMEN CELEBRATE '89 –
EXHIBITION
Entrance Hall, Central Library
14th February — 10th March
Details: Birmingham City Council
021-235 2549

ART OF THE CITY 2
Library Exhibition Hall
15th February — 4th March
Details: Birmingham City Council
021-235 3392

ARTS AND CRAFT EXHIBITION
Clock Tower, High Street, Harborne
15th-18th February
Details: Birmingham City Council
021-426 6444

ORCHESTRA DA CAMERA –
KENNETH PAGE
Adrian Boult Hall
17th February
Details: Birmingham School of Music
021-331 5908

WEEKEND FOR WIND PLAYERS
Midlands Arts Centre
17th-19th February
Details: Midlands Arts Centre
021-440 4221

BIRMINGHAM CITY v
MANCHESTER CITY
St. Andrews Ground
18th February
Details: Birmingham City F.C. plc
021-772 0101

BIRMINGHAM BACH SOCIETY
ORCHESTRA
Adrian Boult Hall
18th February
Director/Soloist George Malcolm.
Orchestral Suite No. 2, Brandenburg
Concerto No. 5, F Minor Harpsichord
Concerto
Details: Birmingham Bach Society
021-456 2114

WOMEN'S NATIONAL CROSS
COUNTRY CHAMPIONSHIPS
Senneleys Park
18th February
2,000 women compete in the new
Senneleys Park.
Details: Birmingham City Council
021-235 3008

THE ALBION ENSEMBLE
Midlands Arts Centre
18th February
Details: Midlands Arts Centre
021-440 4221

BOAT, CARAVAN AND
LEISURE SHOW
N.E.C.
18th-26th February
Considered to be one of the largest general
leisure shows in the UK
Details: Birmingham Post & Mail
(Exhibitions) Ltd.
021-233 3958

"AIDA" by G. VERDI
Sutton Coldfield Town Hall
20th-25th February
Details: Royal Sutton Players (Opera)
021-308 4093

BANNERS GATE MUSIC SOCIETY
Highbury Little Theatre
21st-25th February
Details: Highbury Community Theatre
Arts Centre 021-373 1961

CBSO THURSDAY SERIES
Birmingham Town Hall
23rd February
Beethoven — Symphony No. 6 (Pastoral),
Ravel — Suite, Mother Goose, Scriabin —
Poem of Ecstasy. Conductor Gerard
Schwatz
Details: CBSO 021-236 1555

ARIOSO QUARTET SERIES
Birmingham & Midland Institute
23rd February
Joubert Piano Trio, Schubert Piano No. 1
in Bb, Jeremy Ballard (Violin). David
Powell (Cello). Malcolm Wilson (Piano).
Details: The Birmingham and Midland
Institute 021-236 3591

8TH INTERNATIONAL SWIMMING POOL AND LEISURE SHOW
N.E.C.
23rd-26th February
Details: Conference and Marketing
Association 073522 2875

SAXTET
Midlands Arts Centre
24th February
Details: Midlands Arts Centre
021-440 4221

BSM SYMPHONIC WIND ENSEMBLE /BRASS BAND
Adrian Boult Hall
24th February
Details: Birmingham School of Music
021-331 5908

HUNTING GROUP (EXHIBITION FROM LONDON)
RBSA Gallery
24th February — 8th March
Details: Royal Birmingham Society of
Artists 021-643 3768

ASTON VILLA F.C. v CHARLTON ATHLETIC
Villa Park
25th February
Details: Aston Villa Football Club Ltd.
021-328 1722

STAMIC QUARTET (PRAGUE)
Adrian Boult Hall
25th February
Haydn Quartet Op. 74/3 in G Minor.
Janacek Quartet No. 2 'Intimate Letters'.
Beethoven Quartet Op. 95 in F Minor
Details: Birmingham Chamber Music
Society
021-643 7041

WOMEN'S POWER LIFTING CHAMPIONSHIPS
Great Barr Leisure Centre
25th-26th February
Details: Birmingham City Council
021-235 3008

CBSO SATURDAYS AT SEVEN
Birmingham Town Hall
25th February
Ravel — Suite, Mother Goose, Saint-Saens
— Piano Concerto No. 2, Beethoven —
Symphony No. 6 (Pastoral). Conductor
Gerard Schwatz. Soloist Martin Roscoe
Details: CBSO 021-236 1555

THE SERIES
Adrian Boult Hall
26th February
Keith Tippett String Trio, Rova Saxophone
Quartet
Details: Birmingham Jazz 021-414 5703

LUNCHTIME CONCERT SEASON MC PMS
Birmingham Cathedral
27th February
Mendelssohn Piano Quartet in B minor.
Barrie Grayson: "Spring" — Song cycle for
Soprano and Piano Quartet. Catherine
James — Soprano, Midland Piano Quartet
Details: The Midland Chamber Players
Music Society 021-449 2352

CBSO TUESDAY SERIES
Birmingham Town Hall
28th February
Mendelssohn — Overture, Son and
Stranger, Saint-Saens — Piano Concerto
No. 2, Webern — Langsamer Satz,
Schumann — Symphony No. 1 (Spring).
Conductor Gerard Schwarz. Soloist
Martin Roscoe
Details: CBSO 021-236 1555

CONCERT TRAILS / LUDOW PHILHARMONIC PRIZE
Adrian Boult Hall
28th February
Details: Birmingham School of Music
021-331 5908

THE ROYAL BALLET
Birmingham Hippodrome
28th February — 4th March
Programmes include "Romeo and Juliet"
and "Ondine"
Details: Birmingham Hippodrome
021-622 7486

PRIMARY DANCE FESTIVAL
February — March
Details: Birmingham City Council
021-235 2552

BIRMINGHAM GOOD DESIGN INITIATIVE
February
Judging of the International Design
Competition.
Details: Birmingham City Council
021-235 4506

TALLIS SCHOLARS CONCERT
St. Alban's, Conybere Street
February
The leading exponents of Renaissance
choral music and winners of the 1987
Gramophone Award.
Details: Tallis Scholars 0865 244557

"FACE OF THE CITY"
Various community venues
February — March
Community show — When two people
enter a photographic competition they
set out to capture the heart and soul of
their city.
Details: Bread and Circuses Theatre
Company Ltd. 021-786 2096

GRADINGS AND COURSES IN JU-JITSU AND KICK BOXING
Bushido Ju-Jitsu Centre
February — November
Details: Bushido Ju-Jitsu Centre
021-300 6688

March

Diary of events from 2nd – 31st March

**THE JUST SO STORIES –
CANNON HILL PUPPET COMPANY**
Highbury Little Theatre
2nd-4th March
Details: Highbury Community Theatre
Arts Centre 021-373 1961

**BIRMINGHAM SCHOOL OF MUSIC
FESTIVAL FOR THE CENTENARY**
3rd-18th March
Opening Festival Concert
Featuring the World Premiere of
Centenary Firedances by Birmingham
Composer Andrew Downes. The work
has been commissioned by the City to
mark its 100th birthday and long
musical tradition.
Adrian Boult Hall – 7.30pm
Details: Birmingham School of Music
021-331 5908
Midlands Youth Orchestra
Adrian Boult Hall – 7.30pm
4th March
Birmingham Contemporary Music
Group Concert
Vic Hoyland (New Commission)
Adrian Boult Hall – 7.30pm
5th March
Bernard Brown Ensemble Prize
Recital Hall – 3.15-5.00pm
7th March
Fine Arts Brass Ensemble Concert
Adrian Boult Hall – 7.30pm
7th March
BSM Big Band Concert
Recital Hall – 1.00pm
8th March
Orchestra da Camera
with John Wilbraham
Adrian Boult Hall – 7.30pm
10th March
Academy of St. Philips
Adrian Boult Hall – 7.30pm
11th March
Pinsent Celebrity Concert
Alan Schiller Director and Piano Soloist
Adrian Boult Hall – 1.00pm
14th March
Stan Tracey Orchestra presented by
Birmingham Jazz Society
Duke Ellington Arrangements
Stan Tracey – Genesis
Adrian Boult Hall – 7.30pm
16th March
Polytechnic Chorus and BSM
Symphony Orchestra
Dream of Gerontius-Elgar
Birmingham Town Hall – 7.30pm
18th March
Conductor – Roy Wales
Details: Birmingham School of Music
021-331 5908

**RUGBY – MOSELEY v
LONDON IRISH**
The Reddings
3rd March
Details: Moseley Football Club
021-449 2149

**BIRMINGHAM CITY v
OXFORD UNITED**
St. Andrews Ground
4th March
Details: Birmingham City F.C. Plc
021-772 0101

**BIRMINGHAM NETBALL LEAGUE –
BIRMINGHAM v HERTFORDSHIRE**
Great Barr School
4th March
Details: Birmingham Netball League
458 2000 Ext. 3417

**DAY OF PARTICIPATION –
SCOTTISH COUNTRY DANCING**
Edgbaston C. of E. College for Girls
4th March
Details: Royal Scottish Country Dance
Society 021-200 3132

**ENGLISH CLOSED TABLE TENNIS
SENIOR CHAMPIONSHIP**
Aston Villa Leisure Centre
4th-5th March
Details: Birmingham Sports Advisory
Council 021-235 4430

**WEEKEND COURSE: BRAHMS
AND THE PIANO**
Midlands Arts Centre
4th-5th March
Details: Midlands Arts Centre
021-440 4221

**"OUR DAY OUT" by WILLY
RUSSELL**
The Crescent Theatre
4th-11th March
Details: The Crescent Theatre
021-420 5007

WOMEN'S FESTIVAL
Throughout Birmingham
4th-19th March
A kaleidoscope of events to appeal to
women from all backgrounds in the
community – Arts and crafts; health
and fitness; work and training and lots
more.
Details: Birmingham City Council
021-235 2549

**THE FINALS OF THE MIDLANDS
SCHOOLS DEBATING CONTEST**
Birmingham & Midland Institute
6th March
Sponsored by the Birmingham Post,
The Birmingham & Midland Institute
and National Westminster Bank plc.
Details: Birmingham Post
021-236 3366

**MITCHELLS AND BUTLERS BRITISH
JAZZ AWARDS**
Grand Hotel
6th March
The outstanding formal event of the
British Jazz Calendar. The Awards are
presented to the winners of 9 categories
decided by a national poll of jazz fans.
Details: Brum Beat 021-455 9659

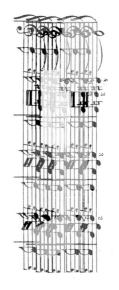

OPERA NORTH
Birmingham Hippodrome
7th-10th March
Programme includes: "For the love of 3
oranges'" "Flying Dutchman," "Aida"
Details: Birmingham Hippodrome
021-622 7486

CBSO THURSDAY SERIES
Birmingham Town Hall
9th March
Mozart: The Marriage of Figaro (Concert
performance in Italian) Conductor
Simon Rattle.
Details: CBSO 021-236 1555

ARIOSO QUARTET SERIES
Birmingham & Midland Institute
9th March
Hindemith: Sonata (Trauermusik),
Schubert: Arpeggione Sonata. Eugen
Popescu-Doreanu (Viola). Joyce
Woodhead (Piano)
Details: The Birmingham and Midland
Institute
021-236 3591

**ASTON VILLA F.C. v
MANCHESTER UNITED**
Villa Park
11th March
Details: Aston Villa Football Club Ltd.
021-328 1722

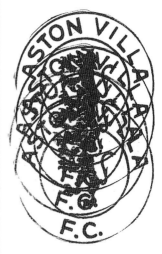

RUGBY – MOSELEY v ORRELL
The Reddings
11th March
Details: Moseley Football Club
021-449 2149

**LEIPZIG CONNECTIONS –
BIRMINGHAM BACH
SOCIETY CHOIR**
St. Paul's Church
11th March
A Capella concert. Including Bach,
Mendelssohn, Reger, Schumann
Details: Birmingham Bach Society
021-456 2114

**PIERS ADAMS (RECORDER) –
NIGEL TILLEY (HARPSICHORD)**
Midlands Arts Centre
11th March
Details: Midlands Arts Centre
021-440 4221

ENGRAVING THEN AND NOW
Museum and Art Gallery
11th March — 9th April
This exhibition celebrates the 50th
anniversary of The Society of Wood
Engravers, founded by Robert Gibbings,
Lucien Pissarro, Eric Gill and others in
1920. Organised by artists, this show
contains over a hundred and fifty past
and current practitioners of a strong
and recently revived print medium.
Details: Birmingham City Council
021-235 2800

**LUNCHTIME CONCERT SEASON –
MCPMS**
Birmingham Cathedral
13th March
Schubert Octet in F for strings and
wind. Midland String Quintet and Wind
Soloists
Details: The Midland Chamber Players
Music Society 021-449 2352

HEALTH WEEK & EXHIBITION
Yew Tree School
13th-18th March
Details: Yew Tree School 021-327 0655

CBSO TUESDAY SERIES
Birmingham Town Hall
14th March
Alexander Goehr; Eve dreams in
Paradise (Premiere, Feeney Trust
Commission). Shostakovich; Symphony
No. 5
Conductor Simon Rattle.
Details: CBSO 021-236 1555

**BIRMINGHAM CITY v
SWINDON TOWN**
St. Andrews Ground
14th March
Details: Birmingham City F.C. plc.
021-772 0101

PINSENT CELEBRITY CONCERT
Adrian Boult Hall
14th March
Alan Schiller Director and Piano Soloist
BSM Ensemble
Details: Birmingham School of Music
021-331 5902

CBSO WEDNESDAY SERIES
Birmingham Town Hall
15th March
Alexander Goehr; Eve dreams in
Paradise (Feeney Trust Commission).
Shostakovich; Symphony No. 5.
Conductor Simon Rattle.
Details: CBSO 021-236 1555

**BIRMINGHAM'S TWIN CITIES –
EXHIBITION**
Central Library
15th-30th March
A display of books and other material
Details: Birmingham City Council
021-235 3392

**SHARD END MULTI-CULTURAL
FESTIVAL**
Shard End Community Centre
16th March
Details: Birmingham City Council
021-747 5485

MULTI-CULTURAL BIRMINGHAM
Alexandra Residential & Social Club
16th March
Details: Birmingham Association of
University Women 021-444 2119

**GRAND EXHIBITION OF
ACTIVITIES**
Quinborne Community Centre
17th-19th March
Details: Quinborne Community
Association 021-427 1374

**BIRMINGHAM FESTIVAL CHORAL
SOCIETY**
Birmingham Cathedral
18th March
J. Haydn — The Passion, The Seven Last
Words of Our Redeemer on the Cross.
Missa Sancti Nicolai. Te Deum
Details: Birmingham Festival Choral
Society 021-430 7639

**INTER-AREA YOUTH SNOOKER
FESTIVAL**
Various Venues
18th March
Details: Birmingham City Council
021-440 6841

CHILINGIRIAN QUARTET
Adrian Boult Hall
18th March
Haydn Quartet Op. 55/2 F minor. Mozart
Quartet K.590 in F. Dvorak Quartet Op.
80 in E
Details: Birmingham Chamber Music
Society 021-643 7041

BIRMINGHAM CITY v WALSALL
St. Andrews Ground
18th March
Details: Birmingham City F.C. plc.
021-772 0101

**BOYS BRIGADE BATTALION BAND
CHAMPIONSHIPS**
Cocks Moors Woods Leisure Centre
18th March
Details: The Boys Brigade 021-359 1866

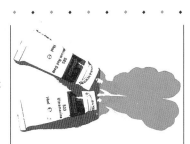

OPEN OIL PAINTING EXHIBITION
RBSA Gallery
18th March — 9th April
Details: Royal Birmingham Society of
Artists 021-643 3768

H. & H. CRAFTS EXHIBITION
Library Exhibition Hall
18th-19th March
Details: Birmingham City Council
021-235 3392

STEAM WEEKEND
Museum of Science and Industry
18th-19th March
Engines from fourteen inches to forty
feet high will be in steam to recreate the
sight, sound and smell of the age of
steam. Engines range from the World's
oldest working steam engine of 1779 to
the Uniflow design of the 1920s
Details: Birmingham City Council
021-235 2800

"STRIPPERS" by PETER TERSON
The Crescent Theatre
18th-25th March
Details: The Crescent Theatre
021-420 5007

MARGARET FINGERHUT (PIANO)
Midlands Arts Centre
19th March
Details: Midlands Arts Centre
021-440 4221

INTRODUCTION TO HOLISTIC HEALTH
Pocklington Place
20th March
Details: Birmingham Rainbow Fellowship 021-777 4050

'YOUNG ARTS' FESTIVAL
City-wide
20th-25th March
Providing a platform for young artists, dancers and musicians to show their skills
Details: Birmingham City Council 021-440 6841

"CANDIDA" G.B. SHAW
Highbury Little Theatre
21st March — 1st April
Details: Highbury Community Theatre Arts Centre 021-373 1961

OPEN DAY
Welsh House Farm Primary School
22nd March
Details: Welsh House Farm Primary School 021-427 4355

INTRODUCTION TO MEDITATION
Fox Hollies Leisure Centre
22nd March
Details: Birmingham Rainbow Fellowship 021-777 4050

ARIOSO QUARTET SERIES
Birmingham & Midland Institute
23rd March
Haydn "Seven Last Words", Quartet, Stephen Beck (Narrator)
Details: The Birmingham and Midland Institute 021-236 3591

THE MAUNDY
Birmingham Cathedral
23rd March
The City of Birmingham will be honoured by the presence of Her Majesty the Queen in its Centenary Year when she visits Birmingham Cathedral for the distribution of the Royal Maundy
Details: The Provost, Birmingham Cathedral 021-236 6323

CBSO THURSDAY SERIES
Birmingham Town Hall
23rd March
Heinz Holliger; Two Liszt Transcriptions, Dvorak; Cello Concerto, Brahms; Symphony No. 2. Conductor Simon Rattle. Soloist Lynn Harrell
Details: CBSO 021-236 1555

ECUMENICAL SERVICE FOR GOOD FRIDAY
Birmingham Cathedral
24th March
Details: The Provost, Birmingham Cathedral 021-236 6323

ASTON VILLA F.C. v WEST HAM
Villa Park
25th March
Details: Aston Villa Football Club Ltd. 021-328 1722

RUGBY — MOSELEY v NOTTINGHAM
The Reddings
25th March
Details: Moseley Football Club 021-449 2149

MIDLAND COUNTIES AAA – OMRON
Sutton Park
25th March
12 Stage Road Relay
Details: Midland Counties AAA 021-773 1631

CITY OF BIRMINGHAM INDOOR BOWLS CLUB FINALS DAY
C.B.I.B.C. Indoor Bowling Club
26th March
Details: Birmingham Bowling Association 021-449 2821

EASTER DAY SERVICES
Birmingham Cathedral
26th March
Details: The Provost, Birmingham Cathedral 021-236 6323

HANDMADE IN BIRMINGHAM – CRAFT FESTIVAL
Edgbaston County Cricket Ground
26th-27th March
Details: Hobby Horse Design and Craft Fairs 0564 775252

BIRMINGHAM CITY v SHREWSBURY TOWN
St. Andrews Ground
27th March
Details: Birmingham City F.C. plc. 021-772 0101

EASTER BONNET PARADE – EASTER TUESDAY
Bull Ring Open Market
28th March
Details: Birmingham City Council 021-622 3452

April
Diary of events from 1st — 29th April

TARMAC SCHOOL OF SPORT
29th-31st March
Run in Birmingham and the Black Country. Three days intensive coaching in netball, gymnastics, judo, badminton and table tennis
Details: Birmingham City Council
021-235 2925

BRITISH INTERNATIONAL ANTIQUES FAIR
N.E.C.
30th March — 5th April
One of the most prestigious antiques fairs in the UK, attracting buyers from all over Britain and as far afield as Australia and Japan.
Details: National Exhibition Centre
021-780 4171

WEEKEND FOR STRING PLAYERS
Midlands Arts Centre
31st March — 2nd April
Details: Midlands Arts Centre
021-440 4221

ENTERPRISE '89
N.E.C.
31st March — 2nd April
Details: Acumex Limited 0202 581144

THE FRANKFURT PROJECT — EXHIBITION
Ikon Gallery
March — April
Ikon's 'Frankfurt Project' will bring to Birmingham work by some of the best young artists working in the City of Frankfurt
Details: Ikon Gallery 021-643 0708

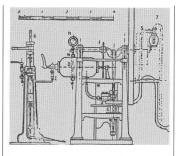

PRIMARY SCIENCE FOCUS EXHIBITION
March
Details: Birmingham City Council
021-235 2552

'CLEAN UP' IN PRIORITY ESTATES
City wide
March
Details: Birmingham City Council
021-454 6001

INNER CITY RESIDENTS CLEAN-UP COMPETITION
March
Details: Birmingham City Council
021-454 6001

STOCKLAND GREEN CENTENARY COMMUNITY PLAY
March
Details: BYV Social Education Programme 021-643 6893

JAZZ EVENING
Four Dwellings School and L.C.
March
Details: Birmingham City Council
021-426 6444

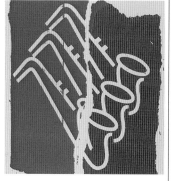

ASTON VILLA F.C. v LUTON TOWN
Villa Park
1st April
Details: Aston Villa Football Club Ltd.
021-328 1722

POST & MAIL CHRISTMAS TREE FUND CENTENARY BALL
Library Exhibition Hall
1st April
Details: Birmingham Post and Mail
021-236 3366

RUGBY — MOSELEY v NEWPORT
The Reddings
1st April
Details: Moseley Football Club
021-449 2149

THE ALLEGRI QUARTET
Midlands Arts Centre
1st April
Details: Midlands Arts Centre
021-440 4221

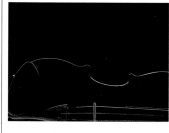

CBSO TUESDAY SERIES
Birmingham Town Hall
4th April
Borodin: Overture, Prince Igor, Prokofiev: Piano Concerto No. 3, Tchaikovsky: Symphony No. 4. Conductor Valery Gergiev. Soloist Eliso Virsaladze
Details: CBSO 021-236 1555

RESTORED DOLLS EXHIBITION
Central Library
4th April — 4th May
Details: Birmingham City Council
021-235 3392

BRATHAY EXPEDITION TO SOUTH CHINA 1988
Library Exhibition Hall
4th April — 4th May
Details: Birmingham City Council
021-235 3392

TEMBA THEATRE COMPANY — MOTHER POEM
Highbury Little Theatre
5th April
Details: Highbury Community Theatre Arts Centre 021-373 1961

CONCERT — ENGLISH STRING ORCHESTRA
Adrian Boult Hall
6th April
Beethoven — Grosse Frise. Barber — Adagio for Strings
Details: English String Orchestra
0905 613525

VITALITE CHAMPIONS ALL GYMNASTICS
N.E.C.
8th April
Spectacular competition between representatives of many of the world's leading gymnastic nations.
Details: British Amateur Gymnastics Association 0753 34171

RUGBY — MOSELEY v LEICESTER
The Reddings
8th April
Details: Moseley Football Club
021-449 2149

BIRMINGHAM CITY v BRIGHTON & HOVE ALBION
St. Andrews Ground
8th April
Details: Birmingham City F.C. plc.
021-772 0101

JOINT NIGHT OPERATION
Sutton Park
8th & 9th April
The Operation is an overnight adventure for hundreds of youth club members. Starts at midnight!
Details: Birmingham City Council
021-440 6841

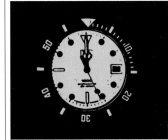

BSM LUNCHTIME CONCERT
Recital Hall
10th April
Details: Birmingham School of Music
021-331 5908

WELSH NATIONAL OPERA
Birmingham Hippodrome
11th-15th April
La Boheme. Il Seraglio. Die Frau ohne Schatten
Details: Welsh National Opera
0222 464 666

CBSO WEDNESDAY SERIES
Birmingham Town Hall
12th April
Haydn: Symphony No. 44 (Trauer), Stravinsky: Concerto in D, Wagner: Siegfried Idyll, Bach: Magnificat.
Conductor Nicholas Kraemer
Details: CBSO 021-236 1555

CONCERT BY ORCHESTRA DA CAMERA
Adrian Boult Hall
12th April
Details: Birmingham School of Music
021-331 5908

INTER-AREA QUIZ
Council House, Victoria Square, Art Gallery
12th & 16th April
Budding 'Brains of Brum' battle for the honours in these ever-popular Quiz finals
Details: Birmingham City Council
021-440 6841

?????????????????
?????????????????
?????????????????
?????????????????
?????????????????
?????????????????
?????????????????
?????????????????

CBSO THURSDAY SERIES
Birmingham Town Hall
13th April
Haydn: Symphony No. 44 (Trauer), Stravinsky; Concerto in D, Wagner: Siegfried Idyll, Bach: Magnificat.
Conductor Nicholas Kraemer
Details: CBSO 021-236 1555

ARIOSO QUARTET SERIES
Birmingham & Midland Institute
13th April
Mendelssohn, Debussy, Chopin, Bach. David Powell (Cello) Malcolm Wilson (Piano)
Details: The Birmingham and Midland Institute 021-236 3591

UMPIRES AND CAPTAINS MEETING
Kynocks Social Club
14th April
Details: Giro Business Houses Cricket League 021-553 0988

SEWING EXHIBITION
N.E.C.
14th-16th April
Details: International Craft & Hobby Fair Ltd. 04252 72711

SPONSORED RINGING OF A PEAL OF STEDMAN CINQUES
St. Martins in the Bull Ring
15th April
St. Martin's Band of Bell Ringers aim to create a new peal of 16 bells to be cast and hung in Centenary year. This will be the first ring of its kind in the world.
Details: St. Martin's Band of Bell Ringers 021-477 4949

BHANGRA DANCE
Sparkhill United Church
15th April
Details: Punjab Culture Centre
021-773 7588

BYRD AND BACH CONCERT
Birmingham Cathedral
15th April
Four-part Mass, Motets and Anthems by Byrd, Bach Cantatas given by Birmingham Cathedral Choir and Cantata
Details: Birmingham Cathedral Choir/ Cantata 021-355 5018

UNITED ANIMALS CHARITIES FAIR
Library Exhibition Hall
15th April
Details: Birmingham City Council
021-235 3392

RUGBY – MOSELEY v WASPS
The Reddings
15th April
Details: Moseley Football Club
021-449 2149

MIDLAND COUNTIES AAA-NIKE
Sutton Park
15th April
National 12 Stage Road Relay
Details: Midland Counties AAA
021-773 1631

ASTON VILLA F.C. v SOUTHAMPTON
Villa Park
15th April
Details: Aston Villa Football Club Ltd.
021-328 1722

ENGLISH BASKETBALL ASSOC. BASKETBALL CHAMPIONSHIPS
N.E.C.
15th-16th April
Sponsored by Carlsberg. The event is a play off competition between the top Clubs in the United Kingdom.
Details: Basketball League Limited
021-308 3505

"PAL JOEY" by JOHN O'HARA
The Crescent Theatre
15th-29th April
Details: The Crescent Theatre
021-420 5007

THE ROYAL SOCIETY OF ST. GEORGE ANNUAL SERVICE
Birmingham Cathedral
16th April
Details: The Provost, Birmingham Cathedral
021-236 6323

COUNTY CHAMPIONSHIP WORCS v LEICS – HOCKEY
Fox Hollies Leisure Centre
16th April
Details: Midland Counties Hockey Association 0564 779101

CENTENARY EXHIBITION BY POLYTECHNIC STAFF
RBSA Gallery
16th-30th April
Details: Royal Birmingham Society of Artists 021-643 3768

BIRMINGHAM CITY-WIDE CHRISTIAN CELEBRATION

City-wide
18th-23rd April
A Christian Celebration of renewal and witness in Birmingham's Centenary year led by Archbishop Desmond Tutu
Details: Organising Committee
021-551 4002

CENTENARY MULTI-CULTURAL FESTIVAL

City-wide
21st-30th April
A celebration of the rich cultural heritage of Birmingham's ethnic minority communities. There will be a wide range of colourful events featuring dance, music, drama, visual arts
Details: Birmingham City Council
021-235 2629

CBSO TUESDAY SERIES
Birmingham Town Hall
18th April
Elliott Carter; Remembrance, and a Celebration of some 100 x 150 notes. Mahler; Symphony No. 7. Conductor — Simon Rattle
Details: CBSO 021-236 1555

BSM LUNCHTIME CONCERT
Recital Hall
19th April
Details: Birmingham School of Music
021-331 5908

CRICKET – WARWICK v LANCASHIRE
County Ground
20th April
Details: Warwickshire County Cricket Club 021-440 4292

CONCERT BY ORCHESTRA DA CAMERA
Adrian Boult Hall
21st April
Details: Birmingham School of Music
021-331 5908

LEAGUE XI v WARWICKSHIRE C.C.
Edgbaston Cricket Club
21st April
Details: Birmingham and District Cricket League 021-772 5774

TOWN TWINNING EXHIBITION
Paradise Circus Complex
21st April-29th April
Displays from Birmingham's twin cities from around the world, Frankfurt, Milan, Lyon, Zagreb, Chang Chun and Zaporozhye.
Details: Birmingham City Council
021-235 3898

PROGRAMME OF ENVIRONMENTAL ACTIVITIES
Various Venues
21st-28th April
Details: The Harborne Society
021-472 3811

AN EVENING OF VICTORIAN SPLENDOUR
Strathallan Thistle Hotel
22nd April
Recreating a superb Civic Banquet hosted in 1896 by the Lord Mayor with music of the time by Tea for Three
Details: Strathallan Thistle Hotel
021-455 9777

BIRMINGHAM CITY v BLACKBURN ROVERS
St. Andrews Ground
22nd April
Details: Birmingham City F.C. plc.
021-772 0101

LOCAL ART & CRAFT EXHIBITION
Clock Tower Community Centre
22nd April
Details: The Harborne Society
021-472 3811

CBIBC v SUSSEX IBC
CBIBC Indoor Bowling Club
22nd April
Details: Birmingham Bowling Association 021-449 2821

MUSIC FOR THE SUN KING
Birmingham Cathedral
22nd April
Vocal and instrumental chamber music from the Court of Louis XIV
Details: Halcyon Ensemble 021-476 2800

"BRAVE ARCHITECTURE" – CENTENARY EXHIBITION

Museum and Art Gallery
22nd April – 25th June

"And Birmingham shall be a famous city, of white stone, full of brave architecture, carved and painted" (Edward Burne-Jones, letter to William Kendrick, 1885).

Burne-Jones's vision may not quite have taken physical shape, but the later 1880s and 1890s did witness a remarkable architectural resurgence in Birmingham.

As a contribution to the City Centenary, Birmingham Museum and Art Gallery, is mounting an exhibition of architectural medals and topographical drawings of the City's most important Victorian buildings.

The exhibition will coincide with the Victorian Society's launch of a Conservation Prize and its publication of a booklet of Birmingham walks.
Details: Birmingham City Council 021-235 2800

CRICKET – WARWICKSHIRE v LANCASHIRE

County Ground
23rd April
Details: Warwickshire County Cricket Club 021-440 4292

CRICKET – WARWICKSHIRE v NORTHAMPTONSHIRE

County Ground
25th April
Details: Warwickshire County Cricket Club 021-440 4292

CRICKET – WARWICKSHIRE v WORCESTERSHIRE

County Ground
27th April
Details: Warwickshire County Cricket Club 021-440 4292

ARIOSO QUARTET SERIES

Birmingham & Midland Institute
27th April
Puccini "Crisantemi" Quartet, Schubert Quintet in C with Ulrich Heinen (Cello)
Details: The Birmingham and Midland Institute 021-236 3591

PHILHARMONIA ORCHESTRA

Birmingham Town Hall
27th April
Vaughan Williams – Symphony No. 6, Brahms – Symphony No. 4. Conductor Andrew Davis
Details: CBSO 021-236 1555

MARRIAGE OF FIGARO/MOZART – BSM OPERA

Adrian Boult Hall
27th-30th April
Details: Birmingham School of Music 021-331 5908

LUNCHTIME CONCERT SEASON – MCPMS

Birmingham Cathedral
28th April
Mozart: Oboe Quartet in F. Benjamin Britten: Fantasy Quartet Julie Robinson (Oboe). Midland String Trio
Details: The Midland Chamber Players Music Society 021-449 2352

RAYMOND MASON: SCULPTURE & DRAWINGS CENTENARY EXHIBITION

Museum and Art Gallery
28th April – 18th June

Mason's vigorous figurative sculptures aroused critical controversy and public enthusiasm when they were shown in the UK for the first time in 1981/82. This show will be a major retrospective and the sculptor's first exhibition in his native city.

Mason is currently working on his first major public sculpture in Britain. This is a crowd scene for Birmingham's new International Convention Centre.

After opening in Birmingham the exhibition will tour to Manchester and Edinburgh. A film currently being made by Central Television (Contrasts, Jim Berrow – Producer, Catherine Collis – Director) will tour with the exhibition.

Illustrated catalogue (Lund Humphries). Supported by the Arts Council of Great Britain, the Marlborough Gallery and the Henry Moore Foundation.
Details: Birmingham City Council 021-235 2800

ASTON VILLA F.C. v MIDDLESBROUGH

Villa Park
29th April
Details: Aston Villa Football Club Ltd. 021-328 1722

REGIONAL JUNIOR SNOOKER

Fisher & Ludlow Social Club
29th April
Details: British Sports Association 021-354 5369

PHOTOGRAPHY EXHIBITION

N.E.C.
29th April – 1st May
Details: Jessop of Leicester 0533 320033

BRMB WALKATHON

Outer circle of the City
30th April
More than 30,000 participants walk 25 miles raising in excess of £300,000 for charity
Details: BRMB Radio 021-359 4481

May
Diary of events from 1st — 31st May

THE NATIONAL CLASSIC MOTOR SHOW
N.E.C.
29th April — 1st May
The country's largest indoor exhibition of classic and historic cars with some 600 vehicles housed in two of the NEC's halls. Sponsored by Classic Cars Magazine.
Details: Cahners Exhibitions Ltd. 01-948 9800

FULL LEAGUE CRICKET PROGRAMME
Various venues
April — September
Details: Giro Business House Cricket League 021-553 0988

LITTERMONSTER COMPETITION
City wide
April
Schoolchildren throughout the City are invited to build their own 'Monster' from waste paper
Details: Birmingham City Council 021-454 6001

CENTRAL HEARTBEAT GALA FASHION SHOW
Grand Hotel
April
Featuring the work of local and national fashion designers supported by West Midlands business
Details: Central Heartbeat 021-472 2294

SPECIAL EVENTS DAYS
Midland Bus & Transport Museum
April — November
Special event days will be held on the first Sunday each month and holiday Sundays and Mondays.
Details: Midland Bus and Transport Museum 0543 253941

CENTENARY "KNOW YOUR BIRMINGHAM" QUIZ
April — June
Sponsored by the Birmingham Post & Mail
Details: Junior Chamber Birmingham 021-454 6171

BIRMINGHAM NETBALL LEAGUE – END OF SEASON TOURNAMENT
Chamberlain Gardens
April — May
Details: Birmingham Netball League 021-458 2000 Ex 3417

BIRMINGHAM CITY v BRADFORD CITY
St. Andrews Ground
1st May
Details: Birmingham City F.C. plc. 021-772 0101

MAY DAY CELEBRATIONS
Trades Union Study Centre
1st May
Talks on Labour History in Birmingham over the last 100 years and Exhibitions
Details: Birmingham May Day Committee 021-236 0735

"LA CAGE AUX FOLLES" STARRING DANNY LA RUE
Alexandra Theatre
1st May — 10th June
Details: Alexandra Theatre 021-643 1231

CBSO TUESDAY SERIES
Birmingham Town Hall
2nd May
Bernd-Alois Zimmermann, Ballet, Roi Ubu, Mahler (orch. Berio); Early Songs, Berlioz; Symphonie Fantastique. Conductor Simon Rattle. Soloist Willard White, bass
Details: CBSO 021-236 1555

"WHY ME?" – by STANLEY PRICE
Highbury Little Theatre
2nd-13th May
Details: Highbury Community Theatre Arts Centre 021-373 1961

LUNCHTIME CONCERT
Recital Hall
3rd May
Music of John McCabe 50th Birthday
Details: Birmingham School of Music 021-331 5908

VICTORIAN DAY
St. Laurence C. of E. Infant School
3rd May
Details: St. Laurence C. of E. Infant School 021-475 1206

SYLVIA CLEAVER CHAMBER MUSIC COMPETITION
Adrian Boult Hall
4th May
Details: Birmingham School of Music 021-331 5908

CENTENARY CELEBRATION QUIZ
Quinborne Community Centre
5th May
Details: Quinborne Community Association 021-427 1374

BSM SYMPHONIC WIND ENSEMBLE
Adrian Boult Hall
5th May
Details: Birmingham School of Music 021-331 5908

NATIONAL DOG SHOW
Perry Park
5th-7th May
One of four certified shows giving entry to Crufts.
Details: Birmingham City Council 021-235 3008

"MUSICAL MEMORIES"
Hall Green Baptist Church
6th May
In aid of the Birmingham Children's Hospice
Details: The Springfield Singers 021-745 1998

CBSO BIRMINGHAM CENTENARY FESTIVAL CONCERT
Birmingham Town Hall
6th May
Birmingham's world famous orchestra, under its conductor Simon Rattle, gives a Gala performance to celebrate the Centenary. The programme includes works by two great names in American music, Gershwin and Bernstein, and by Britain's Peter Maxwell Davies.
Evening performance: 7pm.
Matinee: 2.30pm.
Details: CBSO 021-236 1555

INTER AREA SWIMMING GALA
Nechells Swimming Baths
6th May
Details: Birmingham City Council 021-440 6841

BIRMINGHAM CITY v HULL
St. Andrews Ground
6th May
Details: Birmingham City F.C. plc.
021-772 0101

BHANGRA DANCE
Chamberlain Square
6th May
Details: Punjab Culture Centre
021-773 7588

MARK ANTHONY BARONI (PIANO)
Midlands Arts Centre
7th May
Details: Midlands Arts Centre
021-440 4221

EXHIBITION OF WORK by COLIN SIMMONS & TONY MILLER
RBSA Gallery
7th-20th May
Details: Royal Birmingham Society of Artists 021-643 3768

VINCENT LIEDER COMPETITION
Recital Hall
9th May
Details: Birmingham School of Music
021-331 5908

ALL ABOUT BIRMINGHAM'S VICTORIA SQUARE EXHIBITION
Central Library
9th May — 1st June
Details: Birmingham City Council
021-235 3392

BOURNVILLE COLLEGE OPEN DAY
Bournville College
10th May
Details: Bournville College 021-411 1414

BSM LUNCHTIME CONCERT
Recital Hall
10th May
Details: Birmingham School of Music
021-331 5908

CRICKET – WARWICKSHIRE v SCOTLAND
County Ground
11th May
Details: Warwickshire County Cricket Club 021-440 4292

THE MASK OF TIME – TIPPETT
Birmingham Town Hall
11th & 13th May
Conductor Christopher Robinson. Soloists Faye Robinson, Robert Tear, Sarah Walker, David Wilson-Johnson. The Choir of St. Georges Chapel, Windsor Castle. City of Birmingham Symphony Orchestra. City of Birmingham Choir
Details: City of Birmingham Choir
021-353 8147

MUSIC OF MICHAEL TIPPETT
Adrian Boult Hall
12th May
BSM Chamber Choir. Symphonic Wind Ensemble. Brass Band. Symphony Orchestra. Polytechnic Chorus
Details: Birmingham School of Music
021-331 5908

LUNCHTIME CONCERT – MCPMS
Birmingham Cathedral
12th May
Brahams Piano Quintet in F minor. Midland Piano Quintet
Details: The Midland Chamber Players Music Society 021-449 2352

ONE HUNDRED STEPS FORWARD – CENTENARY EXHIBITION
Museum and Art Gallery
12th May — 31st December
One hundred objects, one for each year of the City's one hundred years, and chosen to represent a significant event of that year, will be on show in the Museum and Art Gallery. The events may be associated with the achievements of individuals, institutions, changes in amenities and the built environment. The majority of objects will be chosen from the Museum's local collections
Details: Birmingham City Council
021-235 2800

NORTHFIELD MUSIC & SPOKEN WORD COMPETITION
Turves Green Girls School
13th May
Details: Mrs. J. Smith 021-476 4741

INDOOR CRICKET FINALS
Strikers Cricket Centre
13th May
For teams of young people from all over Birmingham
Details: Birmingham City Council
021-440 6841

CONCERT OF ENGLISH CHORAL MUSIC
Birmingham Cathedral
13th May
Including Vaughan Williams Mass in G minor
Details: Birmingham Singers
021-743 2347

MIDLAND OPEN TRAMPOLINE CHAMPIONSHIPS
Cocks Moors Woods Leisure Centre
13th May
Details: British Trampoline Federation
0533 810863

ASTON UNIVERSITY AGM OF CONVOCATION AND OPEN DAY
Aston University
13th May
Details: Aston University
021-359 3611 x 4827

ASTON VILLA F.C. v COVENTRY CITY
Villa Park
13th May
Details: Aston Villa Football Club Ltd.
021-328 1722

SUPREME CAT SHOW
N.E.C.
13th May
Details: Governing Council of the Cat Fancy 0278 427575

CHILDREN'S BOOK WEEK
Central and Branch Libraries
13th-20th May
Details: Birmingham City Council
021-235 2175 or 235 3392

STEAM FESTIVAL AND MODEL RAILWAY EXHIBITION
St. Paul's Church
14th May
Details: St. Paul's Church, Birmingham
021-427 5141

THE SERIES
Adrian Boult Hall
14th May
Simon Holt — Kites. Webern — Concerto Op. 24. Colin Matthews — New Commission. Henze — Kammermusik. Conductor Peter Donohoe. Tenor — Nigel Robson
Details: Birmingham Contemporary Music Group 021-236 1555

TRACTION ENGINE RALLY
Museum of Science and Industry
14th May
Details: Birmingham City Council
021-235 2800

BOYS BRIGADE BATTALION PARADE SERVICE
Birmingham Town Hall
14th May
Details: The Boys Brigade 021-359 1866

LORD MAYOR'S FOOTBALL FESTIVAL
Fox Hollies Leisure Centre
14th May
Inter Area Football Competition
Details: Birmingham City Council
021-235 2925

THE CENTENARY MAYOR-MAKING CEREMONY
Birmingham Town Hall
16th May
The inauguration of the new Lord Mayor is the City's premiere civic ceremony, held in the traditional splendour of the Birmingham Town Hall.
Details: Birmingham City Council
021-235 2040

WINIFRED MICKLAM PRIZE
Adrian Boult Hall
16th May
Details: Birmingham School of Music
021-331 5908

PEACE – CHILDREN'S OPERA
CITY OF BIRMINGHAM TOURING OPERA
Midlands Arts Centre
16th-20th May
Peace was commissioned by opera director, Graham Vick. It is rooted in the play THE PEACE by Aristophanes, and uses principal singers and 66 children. It is a non-political, anti-war statement and contains a number of original 'hit' songs. Highly dramatic and also very funny, it is almost certainly the best young people's opera/musical around.
Details: City of Birmingham Touring Opera 021-440 5832

BSM LUNCHTIME CONCERT
Adrian Boult Hall
17th May
Sinfonia/Cont. Music Group
Details: Birmingham School of Music
021-331 5908

BSM CHAMBER ORCHESTRA
Adrian Boult Hall
19th May
Jacqueline Ross. Polytechnic Chorus. Andrew Lloyd Webber — Requiem
Details: Birmingham School of Music
021-331 5908

BACH: MASS IN B MINOR
Adrian Boult Hall
20th May
Tracey Chadwell — Soprano, Nigel Short — Counter-Tenor, John Mark Ainsley — Tenor, Quentin Hayes — Bass. Conductor — Richard Butt
Details: Birmingham Bach Society Choir
021-456 2114

100 YEARS OF COUNCIL SERVICES FESTIVAL
Victoria Square and Chamberlain Square
20th May
A celebration of municipality — past, present and future. A look back at where "The Council" first began, how it then developed into Britain's largest city authority and the plans for the future.
Details: Birmingham City Council
021-235 4469

CRICKET – WARWICKSHIRE v SURREY
County Ground
20th May
Details: Warwickshire County Cricket Club 021-440 4292

WEOLEY CASTLE CARNIVAL
Weoley Castle
20th May
Details: Birmingham City Council
021-477 6261

JUNIOR NIGHT OPERATION
Sutton Park
20th & 21st May
A junior version of the April Senior event
Details: Birmingham City Council
021-440 6841

REGIONAL JUNIOR ATHLETICS
Wyndley Leisure Centre
21st May
Details: British Sports Association
021-354 5369

THE KABADDI GAMES
Ward End Park
21st May
Details: Birmingham City Council
021-327 4505

COMPOSERS PLATFORM, WEST MIDLANDS
Birmingham Town Hall
21st May
Brian Ferneyhough — La Terre est un Homme, Vic Hoyland — In Transit, Jonathan Harvey — Inner Light III. Symphony Orchestra of Composers Platform West Midlands, Paul Venn — Conductor, Jonathan Harvey — Electronics.
Details: Composers Platform of West Midlands 021-449 6786

ST. PAUL'S SPRING MUSIC WEEK
St. Paul's Church
21st-28th May
A varied programme of concerts, choral evensongs and exhibitions.
Details: St. Paul's Church, Birmingham
021-427 5141

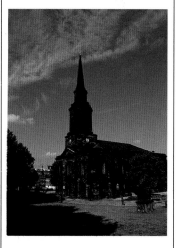

ARTIST IN RESIDENCE – PAM SKELTON
Museum and Art Gallery
22nd May – 2nd July
Pam Skelton is one of the leading artists who has committed herself to living and working in Birmingham. She works in saturated acrylic colours, predominantly on a large scale. Her overriding theme is the archaeological structure of our culture, past and present
Details: Birmingham City Council 021-235 2800

BIRMINGHAM CENTENARY – THE MUSICAL
Midlands Arts Centre
22nd-26th May
A specially written musical entertainment celebrating 100 years of city life. The Company will be working with pupils from schools all over Birmingham.
Details: Big Brum Theatre in Education Company 021-440 2087

YEW TREE FESTIVAL
Yew Tree School
23rd-25th May
Details: Yew Tree School 021-327 0655

MAY FESTIVAL
St. Philip & St. James Church
24th May
Details: Bromford Infant School 021-783 2189

MAY FESTIVAL
Kings Norton J.I. School
24th May
Details: Kings Norton J.I. School 021-458 2411

EXHIBITION & DEMONSTRATION OF COOKERY
St. Benedicts Road
24th May
Details: St. Benedict's Infant School 021-772 0087

CANOE MARATHON – CARDIAC MONITORING APPEAL
N.E.C.
24th May – 4th June
Details: West Midlands Ambulance Brigade 0384 455644

LUNCHTIME CONCERT SEASON – MCPMS
Birmingham Cathedral
26th May
Beethoven Variations Op. 44. Dvorak Piano Trio in E minor "Dumky". Midland Piano Trio.
Details: The Midland Chamber Players Music Society 021-449 2352

HOMES EXHIBITION
N.E.C.
26th May – 4th June
Details: Angex Limited 01-222 9341

MITCHELLS & BUTLERS CENTENARY LORD MAYOR'S SHOW
City Centre
27th May
Everything is new about this event organised by Junior Chamber. The Show will follow a new route, with 100 illuminated floats, 20 marching bands, street entertainers, a fun fair and street markets with a firework display as a spectacular finale
Details: Junior Chamber Birmingham 021-454 6171

BIRMINGHAM SCHOOLS' CONCERT ORCHESTRA
Adrian Boult Hall
27th May
Combination of classical, film and show music
Details: Birmingham Schools' Concert Orchestra 021-440 4111

OPEN WATERCOLOUR EXHIBITION
RBSA Gallery
27th May – 25th June
Details: Royal Birmingham Society of Artists 021-643 3768

CRICKET – WARWICKSHIRE v MIDDLESEX
County Ground
27th-28th May
Details: Warwickshire County Cricket Club 021-440 4292

BRMB WALKATHON
Outer circle of the City
28th May
More than 30,000 participants walk 25 miles raising in excess of £300,000 for charity
Details: BRMB Radio 021-359 4481

CRICKET – LANCS OR WARKS v AUSTRALIA
County Ground
31st May
Details: Warwickshire County Cricket Club 021-440 4292

CENTENARY POETRY COMPETITION – CLOSING DATE
31st May
Details: The Birmingham and Midland Institute 021-236 3591

TEDDY BEARS PICNIC
Cotteridge Junior & Infants School
May
Details: Cotteridge School Parents Association 021-459 0150

LAUNCH OF CITY OF BIRMINGHAM ROSE
Chelsea Flower Show
May
The City has commissioned a rose to commemorate the Centenary. After its launch at the Chelsea Flower Show, it will be planted in parks and gardens around Birmingham.
Details: Birmingham City Council 021-235 2004

CENTENARY FUN DAY ON WHEELS
Birmingham Wheels Project
May
Details: Birmingham City Council 021-359 4314

OPEN DAY
Lindsworth School
May
Details: Lindsworth School 021-444 5211

OPERA WORKSHOP
May
Details: Midland Music Makers Grand Opera Society 021-308 4093

SCHOOL REUNION
Cotteridge Junior & Infants School
May
Details: Cotteridge School Parents Association 021-459 0150

SPRINGERS FUN-DAY
Lee Bank J. & I. School
May
Details: Centenary Committee from the Woodview Estate 021-426 3500

LANGUAGE FAIR
May
Details: Birmingham City Council 021-235 2552

June

Diary of events from 2nd — 30th June

LORDS TAVERNERS INDOOR CRICKET FINALS
Aston Villa Leisure Centre
2nd June
Details: Birmingham City Council
021-235 2925

PERFORMANCE OF "AFRICAN SANCTUS"
Birmingham Town Hall
3rd June
Performance of African Sanctus — David Fanshaw; with Birmingham Choral Union. 'Kokuma Performing Arts' and their Musicians, Theresa Lister — Soprano. Conductor — Colin Baines
Details: Birmingham Choral Union
021-475 5565

CRICKET – WARWICKSHIRE v SUSSEX
County Ground
3rd June
Details: Warwickshire County Cricket Club 021-440 4292

BIRMINGHAM CENTENARY FESTIVAL OF KITES
Cofton Park
3rd-4th June, 11am-5pm
The first of a biennial festival of kite flying, this event will feature a 100 years of kite flying with historic kites, together with displays from all over Europe, stunt kites and Britain's longest serpent kite (500 metres).
Details: Midlands Kite Fliers
021-706 1302

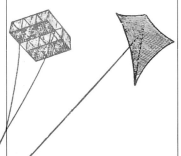

WARWICKSHIRE .22 PISTOL CHAMPIONSHIPS
City of Birmingham and IMI Ranges
3rd & 4th June
Details: Warwickshire Smallbore Rifle & Pistol Assoc. 021-359 4172

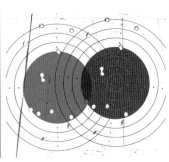

SHEEP SHEARING AND WOOLCRAFTS EVENT
Birmingham Nature Centre
4th June
Details: Birmingham City Council
021-235 2800

CENTENARY DAY
Midland and Bus Transport Museum
4th June
Entire day's services will be operated completely by Historic Birmingham City buses
Details: Midland Bus and Transport Museum 0543 253941

CRICKET – WARWICKSHIRE v SUSSEX
County Ground
4th June
Details: Warwickshire County Cricket Club 021-440 4292

8TH ROYAL SUTTON FUN RUN
Sutton Coldfield
4th June
At least 6,000 participants from 3 weeks to 78 years. Nearly 100 Wheelchair participants
Details: Roy Spare 021-355 1112

"HOBSON'S CHOICE" by HAROLD BRIGHOUSE
Highbury Theatre
6th-17th June
Details: Highbury Community Theatre Arts Centre 021-373 1961

BIRMINGHAM CALLIGRAPHY SOCIETY DISPLAY
Central Library
6th-29th June
Details: Birmingham City Council
021-235 3392

PAINTING ON CHINA
Moat House AEC and Central Library
6th-29th June
Details: Birmingham City Council
021-235 4302

MIDLAND BUS MUSEUM EXHIBITION
Central Library
6th-29th June
Details: Birmingham City Council
021-235 3392

PIANOFORTE COMPETITION
Josiah Mason Hall
8th-9th June
Robert William and Florence Amy Brant Pianoforte Competition — Preliminary and Semi-Finals Stage
Details: Birmingham School of Music
021-331 5902

THE MILK RACE

Finish City Centre
10th June
The final stage of the country's premier cycling event once again comes to Birmingham
Details: Birmingham City Council
021-235 3008

WOODGATE VALLEY COMMUNITY ACTIVITIES WEEKEND
Woodgate Valley
10th June
Details: Birmingham City Council
021-477 6261

CBSO SATURDAYS AT SEVEN
Birmingham Town Hall
10th June
Tchaikovsky; Overture, Romeo and Juliet, Strauss; Oboe Concerto, Dvorak; Symphony No. 8 in G. Conductor — Jiri Belohlavek. Soloist — Richard Weigall
Details: CBSO 021-236 1555

YOUTH FESTIVAL
City Wide
10th June — 8th July
Details: Birmingham Young Peoples Council 021-444 4148

SUMMER FETE
Sylvington Close, Middle Park Estate
10th June
Details: Middle Park Residents Association 021-476 1210

"WHEN WE ARE MARRIED" by J.B. PRIESTLEY
The Crescent Theatre
10th-24th June
Details: The Crescent Theatre
021-420 5007

GREAT MIDLAND BIKE RIDE
Cannon Hill Park
11th June
Details: Cancer Research Campaign
021-471 1235

CELEBRITY SHOW – AM GOLF TOURNAMENT
Cocks Moors Woods Leisure Centre
11th June
Famous names from the world of entertainment play golf for Charity
Details: Central Heartbeat
021-472 2294

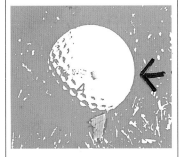

ENGLISH SCHOOLS FOOTBALL UNDER 15 v WEST GERMANY
Alexander Stadium
12th June
Details: Birmingham City Council
021-235 2925

"IMAGES OF CHANGE" EXHIBITION AND BOOK
Library Exhibition Hall
12th-16th June
100 years of Birmingham as seen by the youth of today.
Details: Birmingham City Council
021-235 2552

DOW CLASSIC – TENNIS TOURNAMENT
Edgbaston Priory Tennis Club
12th-18th June
One of the major Ladies' Tournaments in the run-up to Wimbledon
Details: Edgbaston Priory Tennis Club
021-440 2492

EXHIBITION OF CERAMICS
Various venues
12th-29th June
Details: Birmingham Institute of Art and Design 021-331 5777

CRICKET – AUSTRALIA v WARWICKSHIRE or LANCASHIRE
County Ground
14th June
Details: Warwickshire County Cricket Club 021-440 4292

CENTENARY FASHION SHOW
Council House
14th-16th June
Details: Birmingham Institute of Art and Design 021-331 5777

NECHELLS FUN DAY
Nechells
15th June
Details: Birmingham City Council
021-359 4314

SADLER'S WELLS ROYAL BALLET
Birmingham Hippodrome
15th-20th June
The company brings a sparkling programme to Birmingham in Centenary Year, including Snow Queen, Pineapple Poll, Lazarun Choros and Two Pigeons.
Details: Birmingham Hippodrome
021- 622 7486

ROYAL INTERNATIONAL HORSE SHOW
N.E.C.
15th-18th June
The leading riders of today and the champions of tomorrow return to the NEC for this outstanding show
Details: National Exhibition Centre
021-780 4171

LUNCHTIME CONCERT – MCPMS
Birmingham Cathedral
16th June
Mozart and the Italians, Piano Concerto K. 449. Boccherini and Salieri. Dinah Levine — Piano. Midlands Chamber Players
Details: The Midland Chamber Players Music society 021-449 2352

COMMUNITY FAYRE
St. Michael's C. of E. J.I. School
17th June
Details: St. Michael's C. of E. J.I. School
021-554 7818

PIANOFORTE COMPETITION
Adrian Boult Hall
17th June
Robert William and Florence Amy Brant Pianoforte Competition — Final Stage — selected competitors will perform a programme of 40 minutes each
Details: Birmingham School of Music
021-331 5902

BIRMINGHAM FESTIVAL CHORAL SOCIETY CONCERT
Birmingham Cathedral
17th June
Britten — The Building. of the House. Cantata Misericordium. Puccini — Messa di Gloria
Details: Birmingham Festival Choral Society 021-430 7639

WEST HEATH CARNIVAL & FRANKLEY CARNIVAL
17th June
Details: Birmingham City Council
021-477 6261

KINGS HEATH SHOW & CARNIVAL PAGEANT
Various venues
17th June
Details: Kings Heath Community Association 021-444 2277

MIDLAND COUNTIES AAA – OMRON
Alexander Stadium
17th-18th June
Senior Midland Area Championships
Details: Alexander Stadium
021-356 8008

INTER AREA SUPERSTARS FINAL
Cocks Moors Woods Leisure Centre
18th June
Tests of skill and stamina combine to test the best of teams from all Areas of the City
Details: Birmingham City Council
021-440 6841

CRICKET – WARWICKSHIRE v WORCESTERSHIRE
County Ground
18th June
Details: Warwickshire County Cricket Club 021-440 4292

EXHIBITION OF FASHION & TEXTILES

Library Exhibition Hall
20th-25th June
Details: Birmingham Institute of Art and Design 021-331 5777

CRICKET – WARWICKSHIRE v GLAMORGAN

County Ground
21st June
Details: Warwickshire County Cricket Club 021-440 4292

CENTENARY MID SUMMER BALL IN AID OF THE PRINCE'S TRUST

Birmingham Town Hall
22nd June
Details: Birmingham City Council 021-235 2208

SEA CADETS – ROUND BRITAIN '89

23rd June – 8th July
An attempt to break the record for circumnavigating the UK
Details: T. S. Stirling 021-747 6276

BARTLEY GREEN CARNIVAL

Bartley Green
24th June
Details: Birmingham City Council 021-477 6261

BIRMINGHAM KEEP FIT FESTIVAL

Cocks Moors Woods Leisure Centre
24th June
Details: Birmingham Keep Fit Association 021-554 3200

OPEN AIR CENTENARY CONCERT

Cannon Hill Park
24th June
Fireworks music, 1989-style, featuring more than 150 of Birmingham's most talented young musicians.
The Programme will include the second performance of the "Centenary Firedances" to accompany a spectacular firework display across the lake
Details: Birmingham City Council 021-235 4469

SUMMER PROM

Chamberlain Square
24th June
Wander at will from one entertainment to another; listen to the music, watch the dancing – even join in – look at the artists at work
Details: Birmingham City Council 021-235 2208

WARWICKSHIRE FREE PISTOL & AIR PISTOL OPEN CHAMPIONSHIP

IMI and City of Birmingham Range
24th and 25th June
Details: Warwickshire Smallbore Rifle and Pistol Assoc. 021-359 4172

CENTENARY CANAL SIDE FAYRES

City Centre
24th June – 19th August Every Saturday
From the Science Museum to Brindley Place, the canal tow path will be a hive of activity – Craft stalls, artists' displays, entertainment. A great day out for the family
Details: Birmingham City Council 021-235 4502

REGIONAL SENIOR ATHLETICS

Wyndley Leisure Centre
25th June
Details: British Sports Association 021-354 5369

WELSH NATIONAL OPERA

Birmingham Hippodrome
26th June – 1st July
La Sonambula. Ariadne Auf Naxos. Concert – Osud (Opera by Janacek)
Details: Welsh National Opera 0222 464 666

VICTORIAN MARKET & COURT LEET

Bull Ring
27th-30th June
The highlight of this week will be a Court Leet which will convene in Victorian style on Tuesday 27th June and which will also involve dignitaries from St. Martin's Church
Details: Birmingham City Council 021-622 3452

CRICKET – WARWICKSHIRE v WILTSHIRE

County Ground
28th June
Details: Warwickshire County Cricket Club 021-440 4292

LUNCHTIME CONCERT – MCPMS

Birmingham Cathedral
30th June
Schubert "The Trout" Quintet. Midland Chamber Players
Details: The Midland Chamber Players Music Society 021-449 2352

MIDLAND OPEN AMATEUR GOLF CHAMPIONSHIP

Little Aston and Sutton Coldfield Golf Clubs
30th June – 1st July
Details: Midland Golf Union 0905 778560

TOWN TWINNING FOOTBALL TOURNAMENT

30th June – 2nd July
Lyon / Milan / Frankfurt and Belfast City Councils have been invited to participate
Details: Birmingham City Council 021-235 3898

THE LEEDS ENGLISH SCHOOLS TABLE TENNIS INTERNATIONAL

Stockland Green Leisure Centre
30th June – 2nd July
Details: Birmingham City Council 021-235 2925

PICNIC & TEA CONCERT FOR SENIOR CITIZENS

Bromford Infant/Junior School
June
Details: Bromford Infant School 021-783 2189

SUMMER FETE

Lindsworth School
June
Details: Lindsworth School 021-444 5211

RECYCLING OF WASTE FOR CHARITY – COMPETITION

June
Details: Birmingham City Council 021-454 6001

"MUSIC ALIVE" MUSIC FESTIVAL

Blue Coat School
June – July
Details: Birmingham City Council 021-426 6466

PRIMARY SCHOOLS MUSIC FESTIVAL

June
Details: Birmingham City Council 021-235 2552

July
Diary of events from 1st — 30th July

SUMMER FAYRE & FUN DAY
Four Dwellings Centre
2nd July
Details: Four Dwellings Centre
021-422 1066

REGIONAL SENIOR SNOOKER
Fisher & Ludlow Social Club
2nd July
Details: British Sports Association
021-354 5369

BRITISH BOWLING ASSOC. PRESIDENTS DAY
W.M. Police Sports Ground
2nd July
Details: Birmingham Bowling
Association 021-449 2821

CATHEDRAL INTERNATIONAL SUMMER SCHOOL
Birmingham Cathedral
3rd-30th July
Details: The Provost, Birmingham
Cathedral 021-236 6323

MARKETS YOUNG JAZZ MUSICIAN OF THE YEAR COMPETITION
4th July
Details: Birmingham City Council
021-622 3452

BIRMINGHAM MODEL DISPLAY TEAM EXHIBITION
Central Library
4th-27th July
Details: Birmingham City Council
021-235 3392

CRICKET – AUSTRALIA 3RD TEST
County Ground
6th — 11th July
Details: Warwickshire County Cricket
Club 021-440 4292

THE BIRMINGHAM YOUTH SHOW
Birmingham Repertory Theatre
6th-8th July
A foot-tapping feast of song, dance and
comedy by the cream of Birmingham's
young entertainers
Details: Birmingham City Council
021-440 6841

NORTHFIELD CARNIVAL
Northfield
1st July
Details: Birmingham City Council
021-477 6261

ASTON CARNIVAL
Aston Park
1st July
Details: Birmingham City Council
021-359 4314

SUMMERFIELD FESTIVAL
Summerfield Park
1st July
Details: Birmingham City Council
021-454 0863

DAIRY CREST AREA UNDER 20's CHAMPIONSHIPS
Alexander Stadium
1st-2nd July
Details: Midland Counties AAA
021-356 8008

BIRMINGHAM INTERNATIONAL JAZZ FESTIVAL
City-wide
7th-16th July
Once again, Birmingham swings to the
sounds of jazz. 10 solid days of great
music-making — over 200 events at
least 70% of them FREE in venues all
over the City.
This promises to be the best Festival yet
with a host of international stars
playing memorable evenings of world
class jazz.
Details: Brum Beat 021-455 6659

BHANGRA DANCE
Sparkhill Centre
8th July
Details: Punjab Culture Centre
021-773 7588

CENTENARY PERFORMANCE OF ELIJAH
Birmingham Town Hall
8th July
Conductor Rafael Fruhbeck de Burgos.
Soloists — Margaret Marshall (soprano),
Alfreda Hodgson (contralto), Ian Caley
(tenor) and Benjamin Luxon (bass).
CBSO Chorus and CBSO
Mendelssohn's oratorio, Elijah is closely
associated with music-making in the
City, having received its première in
Birmiingham in 1846.
Details: CBSO 021-236 1555

WOODGATE CHURCH CENTENARY FUN DAY
Woodgate Church
8th July
Details: Birmingham City Council
021-477 6261

CENTENARY STREET PARTIES
City-wide
8th July
This is your day for celebrating the
City's Birthday with your own
community Street Parties.
For your do-it-yourself party pack
contact your Area Office
Details: Your Birmingham City Council
Area Office

HANDSWORTH FESTIVAL
Handsworth Park
8th July
Details: Birmingham City Council
021-454 0863

CADER IDRIS & THE CITY OF A THOUSAND TRADES EXHIBITION
Ikon Gallery
8th July — 12th August
Exhibition on heyday of Birmingham's
industry with aspects of the city's
current process of regeneration
Details: Ikon Gallery 021-643 0708

ARTIST'S CHOICE: SIMON LEWTY CENTENARY EXHIBITION
Museum and Art Gallery
8th July – 20th August
Simon Lewty was born in Sutton Coldfield and now lives and works in Leamington Spa. He visited Birmingham Museum as a child, and his selection will represent something of a personal travel through time
Details: Birmingham City Council
021-235 2800

JOINT ATHLETICS MEETING
Wyndley Stadium
9th July
This top meeting gives the chance for young athletes from all Areas of the City to compete for honours at the highest level
Details: Birmingham City Council
021-440 6841

JUBILEE TROPHY DAY
W.M. Police Sports Ground
9th July
Details: Birmingham Bowling Association
021-449 2821

"MADE IN BIRMINGHAM" HISTORIC VEHICLE RALLY
Aston Hall
9th July
Details: Birmingham City Council
021-235 2800

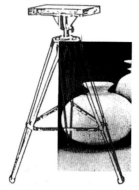

CRAFT WEEK
Yew Tree School
10th-15th July
Details: Yew Tree School 021-327 0655

THE GIRL GUIDES – A CITY CENTENARY CELEBRATION
Birmingham Town Hall
14th July
Details: The Girl Guides Association
021-706 1666

COFTON COMMUNITY ASSOC. CENTENARY OPEN DAY
15th July
Details: Birmingham City Council
021-477 6261

"BRIMSTONE & TREACLE" by DENNIS POTTER
The Crescent Theatre
15th-29th July
Details: The Crescent Theatre
021-420 5007

LORD MAYOR'S YOUTH SPORTS FESTIVAL
Birmingham Sports Centre
16th July
Details: Birmingham City Council
021-235 2925

CRICKET – THE PRINCE OF WALES' XI v THE REST OF THE WORLD XI
County Ground
19th July
Details: Warwickshire County Cricket Club 021-440 4292

YOUTH THEATRE
Highbury Little Theatre
20th-22nd July
Details: Highbury Community Theatre Arts Centre 021-373 1961

THE CENTENARY SUMMER & COUNTRY FAIR
Four Dwellings School
21st July
Details: Four Dwellings Secondary School 021-422 0131

LEY HILL CARNIVAL
22nd July
Details: Birmingham City Council
021-477 6261

SIR HENRY RUSHBURY – CENTENARY EXHIBITION
Museum and Art Gallery
22nd July – 10th September
An exhibition of about 100 etchings, drawings and watercolours, together with books, photographs and memorabilia, celebrates the Centenary of Rushbury's birth. Born in Harborne and trained at the Birmingham School of Art, Rushbury went on to become one of the leading printmakers of his day
Details: Birmingham City Council
021-235 2800

EXHIBITION BY FRIENDS OF THE GALLERY
RBSA Gallery
22nd July – 13th August
Details: Royal Birmingham Society of Artists 021-643 3768

CRICKET – WARWICKSHIRE v SURREY
County Ground
23rd July
Details: Warwickshire County Cricket Club 021-440 4292

CITY OF BIRMINGHAM INTERNATIONAL CENTENARY FOOTBALL TOURNAMENT
Various venues
24th-28th July
Sponsored by Sportsco.
International youth soccer tournament in Birmingham with invited teams from all parts of the U.K. and overseas
Details: Sportsco 0922 649749

CRICKET – WARWICKSHIRE v YORKSHIRE
County Ground
26th July
Details: Warwickshire County Cricket Club 021-440 4292

VICTORIAN WEEK – ACTIVITIES & ENTERTAINMENT
Bells Farmhouse and Bells Farm
26th July – 2nd August
Details: Bells Farm Community Association 021-459 4828

INTERNATIONAL VOLLEYBALL
Aston Villa Leisure Centre
27th-29th July
Details: Birmingham City Council
021-235 3008

FESTIVAL OF BIRMINGHAM
N.E.C. 29th July — 6th August

A spectacular series of exhibitions, concerts and events to celebrate the Centenary of the City of Birmingham.

INDUSTRY AND COMMERCE – 'MADE IN BIRMINGHAM'
An historical look at what has been achieved by the City over the past Century, what is being done today and finally, an exciting and tantalising look at the 21st Century.

CHILDREN'S WORLD
A fun show for 4 to 12 year olds.

YOUTH NOW
A show for the 13 to 18 year olds.

WOMAN TODAY
Valuable advice and assistance to benefit women in their home, family, career and social lifestyles, plus a superb fashion show.

HEALTH DIET AND FITNESS
Definitive advice, assistance, products, equipment and service to help everyone look and feel better, together with an exciting aerobic show.

WATER SPORT SHOW
Information, advice and demonstrations on every conceivable type of water sport.

SPORTS AVIATION
The latest equipment and advice for ballooning, gliding, microlight flying, parachuting, parascending, paragliding etc.

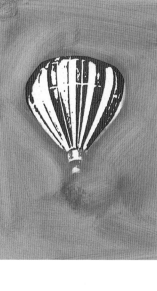

MUSIC FESTIVAL
Virtually every musical style and taste will be featured in a series of live concerts and shows in live performance areas within the National Exhibition Centre.

Top artistes and groups from the world of popular music and rock will join jazz men and classic musicians for what promises to be the musical event of the year. Song contests, Brass and Steel Band competitions together with Reggae, Bhangra Rap and Country music will cover almost every musical taste.

In addition, there will be a Gilbert and Sullivan Operetta, Ballet, , mime artistes, jugglers, strolling players and a series of master classes and clinics.

There will also be a full programme featuring local bands and artistes, a Birmingham band beat contest and a songwriting contest.

Alongside the Festival will be an exhibition of musical instruments.

(Programme subject to confirmation)

FACING YOUR FUTURE
To help everyone over 40 plan ahead for their leisure time and retirement.

GARDEN LIVING
Every conceivable leisure item associated with the garden, from barbecues through wheelbarrows to swimming pools and conservatories.

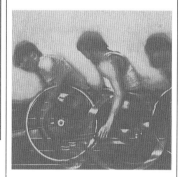

SPORT FOR ALL
A series of games and coaching for children and adults with a special section devoted to disabled sports people. ALSO, the inaugural Birmingham Sporting Championships For full details about these events, contact:-

PINNACLE EVENTS & EXHIBITIONS LTD
Centenary Exhibition Office
47/50 Hockley Hill
Birmingham B18 5AQ
Tel: 021-551 9000
Fax: 021-554 5476

August
Diary of events from 1st – 31st August

MANAV – JANTRA
Midlands Arts Centre
29th July — 12th August
A unique Indian Dance Production.
Workshops and performance
Details: Midlands Arts Centre
021-440 4221

CRICKET – WARWICKSHIRE v GLOUCESTERSHIRE
County Ground
29th-30th July
Details: Warwickshire County Cricket Club 021-440 4292

IT'S A KNOCKOUT & PRIZE GIVING DISCO
Lee Bank J. & I. School
July
Details: Centenary Committee from the Woodview Estate 021-426 3500

AN EXHIBITION OF VICTORIANA
Cromwell J.I. (N.C.) School
July
Details: Cromwell J.I. (N.C.) School
021-359 1012

SCHMIDT ROADSWEEPER COMPETITION
July
Details: Birmingham City Council
021-454 6001

YOUNG SOUNDS GALA CONCERT
July
Details: Birmingham City Council
021-235 2552

BIRMINGHAM CENTENARY BOATING FESTIVAL
July
Details: Brummagem Boats Limited
021-455 6163

FUN DAY
Bromford Infant/Junior Schools
July
Details: Bromford Infant School
021-783 2189

INTERNATIONAL CONFERENCE ON DESIGN & THE CITY
July
In association with the Exhibition of winning schemes of the Birmingham International Design Competition.
Details: Birmingham City Council 021-235 4506

INSPIRED BY ASTON HALL
Aston Hall
1st-11th August
A programme of activities and workshops for children and adults
Details: Birmingham City Council
021-235 2800

N.E.C. AUGUST FAIR
N.E.C.
3rd-6th August
Details: National Exhibition Centre
021-780 4141

BIRMINGHAM COUNTRY MUSIC FESTIVAL
City-wide
4th-13th August
With the grand finale at Cannon Hill Park.
Details: 021-454 7020

BIRMINGHAM BOWLING ASSOC. v DERBY CITY B.A.
6th August
Details: Birmingham Bowling Association 021-449 2821

WOMEN'S AAA NATIONAL CHAMPIONSHIPS
Alexander Stadium
11th-13th August
Details: Midland Counties AAA
021-356 8008

ATHLETICS – COMMONWEALTH GAMES TRIALS
Alexander Stadium
11th-12th August
The cream of English athletes compete for places in the English team for the 1990 New Zealand Commonwealth Games
Details: Birmingham City Council
021-235 3008

CENTENARY PAGEANT – SPONSORED BY THE DAILY NEWS
Cannon Hill Park
4th, 5th & 6th August
A spectacular experience of the City's life and times. This is a new-style entertainment especially devised and produced to celebrate our Centenary, featuring fascinating exhibitions, lavish displays, exciting enactments of incidents from the City's past and tantalising glimpses of our future. Watch entranced as the saga of Birmingham unfolds and our earliest history comes vividly to life; witness the drama of the Civil War and the horror of the blitz; see the rise of industry and the continuing growth of the City as a richly diverse, cosmopolitan and dynamic commercial centre. The Centenary Pageant tells a story of which you are a part — be there and be in it.
Details: Birmingham City Council
021-235 4469

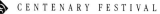
STEAM WEEKEND & 100 YEAR TRANSPORTATION FESTIVAL

Ackers Trust
12th-13th August
Details: The Ackers Trust
021-359 4314

CRICKET – WARWICKSHIRE v SOMERSET

County Ground
12th-13th August
Details: Warwickshire County Cricket Club 021-440 4292

INTRODUCTION TO MEDITATION

Fox Hollies Leisure Centre
16th August
Details: Birmingham Rainbow Fellowship 021-777 4050

EUROPEAN ROLLER SKATING CHAMPIONSHIPS

N.E.C.
17th-28th August
Details: National Exhibition Centre 021-780 4171

CRAFT FAIR

Blakesley Hall
19th-20th August
Details: Birmingham City Council 021-235 2800

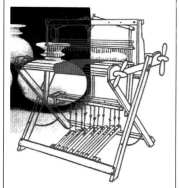

CRICKET – WARWICKSHIRE v DERBYSHIRE

County Ground
20th August
Details: Warwickshire County Cricket Club 021-440 4292

EXHIBITION BY ERNEST HORTON & JOHN RIDOUT

RBSA Gallery
27th August – 10th September
Details: Royal Birmingham Society of Artists 021-643 3768

THE HALFORDS BIRMINGHAM CENTENARY SUPER PRIX

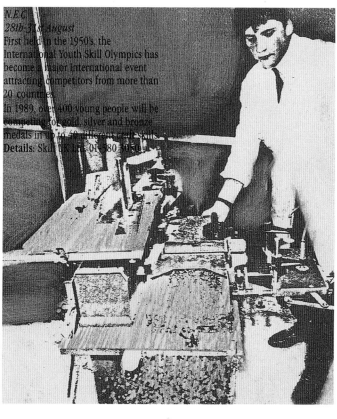

City Centre
27th-28th August
The Halfords Birmingham Centenary Super Prix is Britain's only motor race along city streets. Featuring the 180mph International F3000 Racing Car Championship; the British Saloon Car Championship; the Metro 6R4 Challenge Trophy and a special celebration of 30 years of Mini motoring.

It's two days of super fast motor racing and an action packed festival of entertainment for all the family featuring a childrens fun park, music, dancing, stalls and displays. (Programme to be confirmed)
Details: Birmingham City Council 021-235 2026

SKILL OLYMPICS UK '89

N.E.C
28th-31st August
First held in the 1950's, the International Youth Skill Olympics has become a major international event attracting competitors from more than 20 countries.
In 1989, over 400 young people will be competing for gold, silver and bronze medals in up to 40 different craft skills.
Details: Skill UK Ltd. 01-580 3050

CENTENARY GAME

City-wide
August
An activity designed to help 7-14 year olds get to know their city
Details: Birmingham City Council 021-440 6841

MITCHELLS & BUTLERS CENTENARY STREET PARTIES

August
Details: Mitchells & Butlers Limited 021-236 7766

STREET PARTY

Woodview Drive
August
Details: Centenary Committee from Woodview Estate 021-426 3500

CHILDREN'S TALENT COMPETITION

Bull Ring Open Market
August
Details: Birmingham City Council 021-622 3452

September
Diary of events from 1st – 30th September

CHAMPIONSHIP DOG SHOW
Perry Park
1st-3rd September
The largest outdoor dog show in the world
Details: Birmingham City Council
021-235 3008

GARDENER'S WEEKEND
Kings Heath Park
2nd-3rd September
Major outdoor Garden Show incorporating Central TV Garden
Details: Birmingham City Council
021-235 3008

RSPB CENTENARY EXHIBITION
Central Library
5th-28th September
Details: Royal Society for the Protection of Birds 021-235 3217

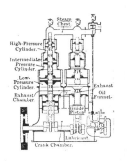

CRICKET – WARWICKSHIRE v NORTHAMPTONSHIRE
County Ground
8th September
Details: Warwickshire County Cricket Club 021-440 4292

MIRFIELD ARTS FESTIVAL
Mirfield Community Centre
8th-9th September
Details: Birmingham City Council
021-783 5898

STATIONARY ENGINE RALLY
Museum of Science and Industry
9th September
Details: Birmingham City Council
021-235 2800

BIRMINGHAM INTERNATIONAL CARNIVAL
Handsworth Park
9th-10th September
The second largest event of its kind in Britain
Details: Birmingham City Council
021-454 0863

SILVER JUBILEE CRICKET MATCH
Holly Lane Sports and Social Centre
10th September
Details: Centre Set Cricket Club
021-354 9052

HARVEST HOME
Birmingham Nature Centre
10th September
Details: Birmingham City Council
021-235 2800

INTER CITY GAMES
Various venues
10th September
Junior Games featuring over 5 sports. Liverpool, Leeds and Salford have confirmed that they are participating
Details: Birmingham City Council
021-235 2925

BIRMINGHAM BOWLING ASSOC. FINALS DAY
W.M. Police Sports Ground
10th September
Details: Birmingham Bowling Association 021-449 2821

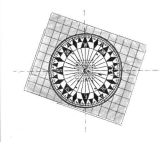

MANAV – JANTRA
The CAVE — 516 Moseley Road
11th-16th September
A unique Indian Dance Production. Workshops and performance
Details: The Cave 021-440 3742

BIRMINGHAM HISTORY CONFERENCE
Adrian Boult Hall
16th-17th September
Details: Birmingham Polytechnic
021-356 6911

CATHEDRAL FESTIVAL WEEKEND
Birmingham Cathedral
16th-18th September
Details: The Provost, Birmingham Cathedral
021-236 6323

COME AND TRY ORIENTEERING
Cannon Hill Park
17th September
Details: Harlequins Orienteering Club
021-382 6168

ART CIRCLE EXHIBITION
RBSA Gallery
17th-30th September
Details: Royal Birmingham Society of Artists 021-643 3768

GALLERY 33 PROJECT

Museum and Art Gallery
21st September

A meeting ground of cultures.

September 1989 sees the opening of an innovative exhibition in Gallery 33. It is about people, our beliefs, values, customs and art. The display draws on the Museum's extensive collection of art and artefacts from the Americas, Africa, Asia and the Pacific.

The exhibition has music and film, a discovery area where visitors can handle objects and some computer games as well as costumes, masks, sculpture and domestic items.

A special feature is the area where musicians, dancers, story tellers and craftspeople can perform.

Details: Birmingham City Council
021-235 2800

BIRMINGHAM CENTENARY VAX MARATHON

24th September

A running extravaganza, featuring a prestige world-class marathon — plus a super headline event to be announced — with prizes totalling £100,000, is expected to draw huge crowds to Birmingham's streets and parks.

Sponsored by Britain's best-selling vacuum cleaner manufacturer, Vax Appliances of Droitwich, the marathon will be run through some of Birmingham's beautiful parks, triggering children's charity fun runs as it progresses.

The event, which is officially supported by the Evening Mail, will feature side shows, street entertainment, hot air balloons and bands in City parks along the route, making it a great day out for all the family.

Amongst the world's richest marathons, it promises to be a magnificent race attracting the very best national and international runners.

The course is being designed by Bud Baldaro, the Tipton Harriers coach, whose squad of long-distance runners is probably the strongest in the country. A fast flat course would place the Centenary Marathon as a leading contender for the Commonwealth Games trial.

Instigated as a major charity fund-raising event, it is anticipated that at least £250,000 will be raised for the NSPCC and Central Heartbeat, the central Birmingham hospitals charity. Sponsors

Vax will start the ball rolling with a promised £10 for every runner crossing the 10 mile mark.

Details: Tim Bosher, Birmingham Centenary Vax Marathon, Carrington Communications, Crusader House, 24 Livery Street, Birmingham B3 2PA
Fax: 021-236 9447.
Tel: 021-236 9458/9466

MIDLAND AIR WEAPON CHAMPIONSHIP

Aston University
23rd & 24th September
Details: Warwickshire Smallbore Rifle & Pistol Assoc. 021-359 4172

ARCHIVES EXHIBITION 1889-1989

Library Exhibition Hall
25th September — 14th October
Details: Birmingham Institute of Art and Design 021-331 5777

THE DAILY MAIL BRITISH SKI SHOW

N.E.C.
28th September — 1st October
Details: Pinnacle Events and Exhibitions 0895 72277

WARWICKSHIRE COUNTY CLOSED CHAMPIONSHIPS – SQUASH

Sutton Coldfield S.C.
30th September — 2nd October
Details: Warwickshire Squash Rackets Association 021-353 2685

2ND BIRMINGHAM INVITATION GAMES FOR THE DISABLED

September
Hosted by the Wobblers and Wheelies and sponsored by Legal and General
Details: Legal and General 021-643 5095

CENTENARY SEASON

Highbury Little Theatre
September
Includes the official opening of redeveloped centre
Details: Highbury Community Theatre Arts Centre 021-373 1961

INTAMEL CONFERENCE

September
Annual Conference of the International Association of Metropolitan Libraries
Details: Birmingham City Council
021-235 4302

BIRMINGHAM FILM & TELEVISION FESTIVAL

Various venues
22nd September — 6th October

One of Britain's most adventurous media events, the Festival's immense variety never fails to impress the critics, connoisseurs and general public alike. It is the only film festival in the UK to cater for small screen buffs as well. "The Festival is a calling card for Birmingham's new image as a media city" — Roger Shannon, Festival Director.

Details: Birmingham Film and Television Festival 021-440 2543

October
Diary of events from 1st – 31st October

HARVEST SONGS OF PRAISE
St. Faith and St. Laurence
1st October
Details: Harborne Council of Christian Churches 021-427 5526

AUTUMN GALA
Birmingham Railway Museum
1st October
Details: Birmingham Railway Museum 021-707 4696

CATHEDRAL FESTIVAL OF DEDICATION
Birmingham Cathedral
1st October
Details: The Provost, Birmingham Cathedral 021-236 6323

SCHOOL OF PLANNING AND LANDSCAPE EXHIBITION
Central Library
3rd-26th October
Details: Birmingham City Council 021-235 4302

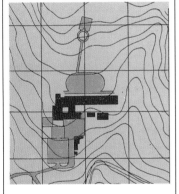

CITY ELDERS CELEBRATE THE CENTENARY
Aston Villa Sports and Leisure Centre
5th October
Our older citizens have a lot to tell us about our City. Over 50 local events in elderly peoples' homes. Lunch clubs and day centres will mount small exhibitions/concerts in Centenary Year. The very best of the local events will be staged at Aston Villa Leisure Centre in a special exhibition "City Elders celebrate the Centenary"
Details: Birmingham City Council/ Arts Link 0782 614170

HARVEST FESTIVAL & SALE OF PRODUCE
Cambridge Road Methodist Church
6th October
Details: Kings Heath Infant School 021-444 0857

HARVEST FESTIVAL & SALE OF PRODUCE
Kings Heath Infant School
6th October
Details: Kings Heath Infant School 021-444 0857

TERCENTENARY OF FREE CHURCH WITNESS
Carrs Lane Church Centre
7th October
Civic Service to celebrate 300 years of free church witness in Birmingham
Details: Birmingham Council of Christian Churches 021-643 6603

ST. ALBAN'S FESTIVAL
St. Alban's, Conybere Street
7th-14th October
Music, dance and drama
Details: St. Alban's Festival Committee 021-440 4034

MEMBERS AND ASSOCIATES EXHIBITION
RBSA Gallery
7th-28th October
Details: Royal Birmingham Society of Artists 021-643 3768

HIKE FOR HEALTH
8th October
Details: Central Heartbeat 021-472 2294

EX CATHEDRA AT ST. ALBAN'S
St. Alban's, Conybere Street
13th October
The first concert of the Choir's 20th Anniversary Season
Details: Ex Cathedra Choir 021-235 2208

MALE VOICE CHOIR CONCERT
Birmimgham Town Hall
14th October
More than 200 voices raised in song. The West Midlands Police Male Voice Choir will be joined by the Bournville, Canoldir and Icknield Male Voice Choirs in a celebration of the City's Centenary
Details: West Midlands Police 021-236 5000 ext. 2405

INDUSTRIAL FESTIVAL EXHIBITION
St. Paul's Church
16th-22nd October
Exhibition of Birmingham's Industry — in conjunction with the Churches Industrial Group Birmingham
Details: St. Paul's Church, Birmingham 021-427 5141

EDUCATION FESTIVAL
City-wide
17th-22nd October
Exhibitions at major sites throughout the City showing the wide-ranging activities of young people in Birmingham's schools and colleges in 1989.
Details: Birmingham City Council 021-235 2552

IMAGES OF A GOLDEN AGE: PAINTINGS FROM SEVENTEENTH CENTURY HOLLAND CENTENARY EXHIBITION

Museum and Art Gallery
7th October – 16th January
This spectacular exhibition, unique to Birmingham, will bring together some 120 works from great public and private collections throughout the UK. It will demonstrate the full range of Dutch painting from the dramatic seascapes of Van de Velde and the landscapes of Ruisdael, Hobbema and Koninck, to the immediacy and psychological complexity of domestic interiors by Vermeer, Pieter de Hooch, Jan Steen, Jakob Ochtervelt and the meticulous Gerrit Dou. Portraiture was the supreme achievement of Dutch seventeenth century art and the works of Rembrandt and Hals will be represented in the show.
Illustrated catalogue by Christopher Wright.
Details: Birmingham City Council 021-235 2800

HEALTH EDUCATION EXHIBITION
St. Laurence Church Junior School
17th-21st October
Details: St. Laurence Church Junior
School 021-475 6499

NATIONAL CHRISTIAN EDUCATION COUNCIL AGM
20th-22nd October
Musical pageant, urban trail for adults
around the older parts of Handsworth
and the Jewellery Quarter
Details: Birmingham Council of
Christian Churches 021-643 1932

"MUSIC OF THE BRITISH ISLES" CONCERT FOR CHARITY
21st October
Details: The Springfield Singers
021-745 1998

STEAM WEEKEND
Museum of Science and Industry
21st-22nd October
Details: Birmingham City Council
021-235 2800

INDUSTRIAL FESTIVAL SERVICE
St. Paul's Church
22nd October
Details: St. Paul's Church, Birmingham
021-427 5141

C.B.I.B.C. v BRIDGEND I.B.C.
C.B.I.B.C. Indoor Bowling Club
22nd October
Details: Birmingham Bowling
Association 021-449 2821

OVER 45 INTER COUNTY CHAMPIONSHIP STAGE I
Sutton Coldfield Squash Club
22nd-23rd October
Details: Warwickshire Squash Rackets
Association 021-353 2685

THE NATIONAL KNITTING EXHIBITION
N.E.C.
26th-29th October
Details: Nationwide Exhibitions (UK)
Ltd. 0272 650465

BIRMINGHAM INTERNATIONAL TATTOO

N.E.C.
28th-29th October
The biggest Tattoo in Britain in 1989.
Programme to include The Band of Her
Majesty's Grenadier Guards, Band of the
Royal Swedish Navy, United States Air
Force Band Europe (Glen Miller's Own),
US Army Berlin Drill Team, The Royal
Signals White Helmet Motor Cycle Team,
Mass Police Pipe and Drum Bands,
Canoldir Choir and other guest bands
and artistes.
Details: Thames Valley Entertainments
0734 575593

BIRMINGHAM INTERNATIONAL MARCHING BANDS CHAMPIONSHIP
N.E.C.
29th October
This event, a first for Birmingham, has
stirred up enormous interest from
leading Marching Bands from all over
the world, twelve of the very best bands,
six from Great Britain and six from
overseas will take part
Details: Thames Valley Entertainments
0734 575593

BIRMINGHAM WATER COLOUR SOCIETY EXHIBITION
RBSA Gallery
29th October — 11th November
Details: Royal Birmingham Society of
Artists 021-643 3768

"SAMSON AND DELILAH" – OPERA
Crescent Theatre, Cumberland Street
31st October — 4th November
Details: Midland Music Makers Grand
Opera Society 021-308 4093

THE 1989 INTERNATIONAL BIKE SHOW
N.E.C.
31st October — 6th November
Details: MCA Exhibitions Ltd.
01-385 1200

BIRMINGHAM UNIVERSITY GUILD OF STUDENTS RAG WEEK
City-wide
31st October — 18th November
Details: Birmingham University Guild of
Students 021-472 1841

A PLAY FOR BIRMINGHAM
Birmingham Repertory Theatre
October
At least 8 of Britain's leading writers are
joining forces to create a play involving
groups all over Birmingham in
celebration of the City's Centenary
Details: Birmingham Repertory Theatre
021-236 4455

'CARING-BINMEN' BALL
October
Details: Birmingham City Council
021-454 6001

SENIOR CITIZENS COMPETITION
October
Details: Birmingham City Council
021-454 6001

HALLOWEEN EVENT
Birmingham Railway Museum
October
Details: Birmingham Railway Museum
021-707 4696

BUSKERS FESTIVAL
All Markets Areas
October
Details: Birmingham City Council
021-622 3452

BIRMINGHAM EDUCATION ARTS FORUM FESTIVAL
Birmingham Hippodrome
October
Cultural Cross Arts Project.
Collaboration of Asian, Afro-Carribean
and European artists based on theme of
work and industry
Details: Birmingham Hippodrome
021-622 7437

SECONDARY SCHOOLS DRAMA FESTIVAL
October
Details: Birmingham City Council
021-235 2552

DEVELOPING THE FUTURE OF THE CITY EXHIBITION
Library Exhibition Hall
October
Details: Birmingham City Council
021-235 4501

November
Diary of events from 2nd — 25th November

49TH BIRMINGHAM MUSIC FESTIVAL
Birmingham and Midland Institute
2nd-4th November
Musical Festival to provide platform for students and amateur musicians to perform in public
Details: Birmingham Music Festival 021-414 6720

THE NATIONAL FESTIVAL OF CRAFTS '89
N.E.C.
2nd-5th November
Details: International Craft and Hobby Fair Ltd. 04252 72711

BONFIRE AND FIREWORK CARNIVALS
City parks
3rd and 5th November
Details: Birmingham City Council 021-235 3008

44TH WORLD CONGRESS OF JCI INTERNATIONAL
Metropole / N.E.C.
5th-11th November
Details: Junior Chamber Birmingham 021-454 6171

EXHIBITION OF BIRMINGHAM ARTISTS
Library Exhibition Hall
6th-18th November
Details: Birmingham Institute of Art and Design 021-331 5777

ASTON HALL BY CANDLELIGHT
Aston Hall
7th-25th November
(Not Sunday and Monday)
Details: Birmingham City Council 021-235 2800

BIRMINGHAM BACH SOCIETY
Adrian Boult Hall
11th November
Details: Birmingham Bach Society 021-456 2114

READERS AND WRITERS FESTIVAL
Midlands Arts Centre
11th-25th November
One of the première events of its kind in the country. There will be workshops and performances by leading poets and authors and a special reading of the winning entry in the Centenary Poetry Competition
Details: Midlands Arts Centre 021-440 4221

CATHEDRAL REMEMBRANCE SERVICE
Birmingham Cathedral
12th November
Details: The Provost, Birmingham Cathedral 021-236 6323

OVER 35 INTER COUNTY CHAMPIONSHIP STAGE I
Centre Square, Pershore Street
12th-13th November
Details: Warwickshire Squash Rackets Association 021-353 2685

MIDLAND PAINTERS EXHIBITION
RBSA Gallery
12th-18th November
Details: Royal Birmingham Society of Artists 021-643 3768

CENTENARY BEAUJOLAIS RUN
Strathallan Thistle Hotel
16th November
"Fun Run" to France and back for charity, the winning post being the Strathallan Thistle Hotel. Sponsored by The Birmingham Post & Mail and Colmore Car Group
Details: Colmore 021-778 2323

B MINOR MASS–BACH EX CATHEDRA
Birmingham Cathedral
18th November
Europe's top Baroque players join Birmingham's top Baroque choir in this celebratory concert
Details: Ex Cathedra 021-235 2208

MIDLAND COUNTIES CAT CLUB CHAMPIONSHIP SHOW
N.E.C.
18th November
Details: Midland Counties Cat Club Bishampton 608

MOZART – REQUIEM
Birmingham Town Hall
18th November
Details: City of Birmingham Choir 021-353 8147

LYON FOOD FESTIVAL
Various venues
19th November
Top chefs from Birmingham's twin city of Lyon under the auspices of Paul Bocuse visit Birmingham to present a gastronomic experience. Master classes and gourmet dinners are just some of the mouth-watering events planned
Details: Caroline Walker Associates 01-584 6045

Paul Bocuse France

EASEL CLUB EXHIBITION
RBSA Gallery
19th-30th November
Details: Royal Birmingham Society of Artists 021-643 3768

UNITED ANIMALS CHARITIES FAIR
Library Exhibition Hall
25th November
Details: Birmingham City Council 021-235 3392

CENTENARY CELEBRATION CONCERT OF ENGLISH MUSIC
Birmingham Cathedral
25th November
J. Rutter — Gloria. Vaughan Williams — Sancta Civitas (Holy City), J. Joubert — "Benedicite", a world premiere, commissioned by the Birmingham Festival Choral Society with funds from City of Birmingham Council. Gunilla Lowenstein — Tellus Mater (Mother Earth)
Details: Birmingham Festival Choral Society 021-430 7639

BIRMINGHAM ARTIST PAM SKELTON'S EXHIBITION
Ikon Gallery
25th November — 6th January
Birmingham artist Pam Skelton's large and colourful paintings will be exhibited to mark her residence at Birmingham City Art Gallery
Details: Ikon Gallery 021-643 0708

SIMON MOLLER EXHIBITION
Ikon Gallery
25th November — 6th January
Using industrial materials and methods, as well as those more traditionally associated with sculpture, Moller works in a surprising number of different metals
Details: Ikon Gallery 021-643 0708

LOMBARD RAC RALLY
Sutton Park
November
See the world's top rally drivers in action.
Details: Birmingham City Council 021-235 3008

MATHEMATICS FAIR
November
Details: Birmingham City Council 021-235 2552

CENTENARY EDITION OF BIRMINGHAM REPORT & ACCOUNTS
November
Available from Council House Reception and libraries
Details: Birmingham City Council 021-235 3107

December

Diary of events from 3rd — 25th December

ADVENT CAROL SERVICE
Birmingham Cathedral
3rd December
Details: The Provost, Birmingham
Cathedral 021-236 6323

INTERNATIONAL CAROL SERVICE
Carrs Lane Church Centre
3rd December
Details: Birmingham Council of
Christian Churches 021-643 6603

WINTER SALON – EXHIBITION
RBSA Gallery
3rd-18th December
Details: Royal Birmingham Society of
Artists 021-643 3768

FINAL OF GENERAL KNOWLEDGE 'BLOCKBUSTER' COMPETITION
Ninestiles School
8th December
Details: Ninestiles School 021-778 1311

NATIONAL EXHIBITION OF CAGE & AVIARY BIRDS
N.E.C.
8th-10th December
Details: Cage and Aviary Birds
01-661 4498

HANDEL'S "MESSIAH"
Birmingham Town Hall
9th & 12th December
Details: City of Birmingham Choir
021-353 8147

BRITAIN'S NATIONAL PIGEON SHOW
N.E.C.
9th-10th December
Details: The Racing Pigeon
021-242 0565
021-780 4141

WENDY RAMSHAW & DAVID WATKINS: NEW JEWELLERY EXHIBITION
Museum and Art Gallery
12th December — 28th February 1990
Wendy Ramshaw and David Watkins are
two jewellers whose innovative uses of
material and continually evolving work
have acted as inspiration to many other
contemporary jewellers.
This exhibition shows an entirely new
group of work now in the process of
being designed and made
Details: Birmingham City Council
021-235 2800

LADIES KENNEL CHAMPIONSHIP DOG SHOW
N.E.C.
15th-16th December
Details: Ladies Kennel Association
045383 2944

CHRISTMAS ORATORIO (COMPLETE) – BIRMINGHAM BACH SOCIETY
Adrian Boult Hall
16th December
Details: Birmingham Bach Society
021-456 2114

CAROLS FOR ALL
Birmingham Town Hall
17th December
The City Choir's traditional contribution
to the Festive Season
Details: City of Birmingham Choir
021-353 8147

"CHRISTMAS MUSIC BY CANDLELIGHT"
St. Paul's Church
22nd and 23rd December
Details: Ex Cathedra 021-235 2208

MIDNIGHT MASS
Birmingham Cathedral
24th December
Details: The Provost, Birmingham
Cathedral 021-236 6323

FESTIVAL OF NINE LESSONS AND CAROLS
Birmingham Cathedral
24th December
Details: The Provost, Birmingham
Cathedral 021-236 6323

CHORAL EUCHARIST FOR CHRISTMAS DAY
Birmingham Cathedral
25th December
Details: The Provost, Birmingham
Cathedral 021-236 6323

SANTA SPECIAL
December
Santa Special 3rd, 10th and
17th December
Details: Birmingham Railway Museum
021-707 4696

NATIVITY AND CAROL CONCERT
Various within Area
December
Details: Centenary Committee from the
Woodview Estate 021-426 3500

'CARE FOR THE ELDERLY' CHRISTMAS PARTY
December
Details: Birmingham City Council
021-454 6001

CENTENARY FINALE – MYSTERY EVENT
City Centre
December
Details: Birmingham City Council
021-235 2208

HALF
NEW FORMU

BEST VALUE
ON THE
ROAD

HALFORDS

▼ A nationwide network of Superstores, ease and convenience of one stop shopping, easy access, free parking, open 7 days a week

▼ Ultra modern shopping environment with the widest range of car parts and accessories anywhere in the UK.

▼ Over 200 models of cycle to choose from, all at guarantee unbeatable prices.**

ORDS
A SHOPPING

nights.†

▼ Complete car service centres offering the best value for money, from 6,000/12,000 mile servicing to fitted accessories, parts and exhausts.

▼ The biggest and best selection for in-car entertainment, hear the best sounds for yourself at our Wall of Sound.

Friendly, helpful and knowledgeable staff able to guide you on selection.

HALFORDS
NO.1 FOR THE ROAD

P TO £400 INSTANT CREDIT* OPEN 7 DAYS A WEEK†

On Sunday 24 September 1989, Birmingham becomes **THE MARATHON CAPITAL OF THE WORLD** and presents **THE BIRMINGHAM CENTENARY VAX MARATHON**

Amongst the
World's richest, with more
than £60,000 in prize money.
Raising at least £100,000 for two great charities.

NSPCC  CENTRAL HEART BEAT

A great day out for all the family.
Entertainment galore in City parks along the
route. Children's charity Fun Runs, hot air
balloons, side shows and bands.

 PLUS

In Cannon Hill Park, a classic head-to-head,
round-the-lakes race between
TWO TRACK SUPERSTARS
(Details to be announced).

Sponsors, Vax Appliances, promise £10 to the
charities for **every** Marathon entrant who crosses
the 10 mile line.
So whether you're a club runner or enthusiastic
amateur, get into training now!

Entry forms and information from:
**The Event Organiser, Birmingham Centenary
Vax Marathon, Carrington Communications,
24 Livery Street, Birmingham B3 2PA.
Fax: 021-236 9447. Tel: 021-236 9458/9466.**

CITY OF BIRMINGHAM CENTENARY FESTIVAL 1889 1989

VAX MARATHON

Making Birmingham
even better
for the next hundred
years...

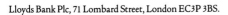

City of memories.

Birmingham, the way we were.

LEFT. THE ENTRANCE TO THE MARKET HALL FROM THE BULL RING. OPENED IN FEBRUARY 1835, THE MARKET HALL LOST ITS ROOF FROM ENEMY AIR ACTION IN THE SECOND WORLD WAR. EVENTUALLY DEMOLISHED, IT WAS REPLACED IN 1964 BY THE PRESENT £8 MILLIONS BULL RING CENTRE.

CENTRE. A BUSY SCENE IN MOAT ROW AROUND 1936 WITH PRODUCE MOVING TO AND FROM THE FRUIT AND VEGETABLE MARKET WHICH EXTENDED UP JAMAICA ROW.

RIGHT. THE BULL RING, BIRMINGHAM'S "SPEAKERS CORNER" COULD ALWAYS MUSTER A GOOD-TEMPERED CROWD OF HECKLERS TO TAKE ON ANY SPEAKER.

In his "Black Country" (1952) Phil Drabble declares that a Black Countryman is insulted to be considered a Brummie, bringing Vivian Bird's riposte in his "Portrait of Birmingham (1970) that a Brummie prefers not to be confused with a Black Countryman. Indeed, with such close proximity the accents differ amazingly, but the deeply-rounded vowels of the Black Country and the flat monotone of Birmingham are matters for the philologist. Accent is an accident of birth. No one suggests that the Aston-born second generation West Indian is a true Brummie though he speaks that vocal caricature beloved of television.

Nor is a woman a Brummie — it is a purely male conception. It may be said of a woman — or a man — that she is "Brummy", but this is a derogatory term smacking of accent allied to crudeness.

So having determined what he is not, what then is a Brummie? Is there a written description of him? William Hutton, Birmingham's first historian, describes the town's inhabitants in 1841: "They possessed a vivacity. I saw men awake; their very step along the street showed alacrity. Hospitality seemed to claim this happy people for her own".

This is scarcely what we regard today as a Brummie. Our Brummie is an amalgam of long experience of the city and his fellow citizens. Unlike the Cockney the Brummie has no Bow Bells qualification, but whatever his suburb he should on a favourable wind hear the distant boom of Big Brum, and with the right humidity have smelt a whiff of chocolate from Bournville. He must have known the cobbled Bull Ring, its stalls, barrow boys, and characters — Tommy Tank the runner; Iron-foot Jack the numerologist; the escapologist in chains; and homburg-hatted Ernie McCulloch, who auctioned ragged boys and bought them clothes.

No one can claim Brummiehood who cannot remember the Market Hall, especially that splendid vista up Station Street of its imposing west front above that array of steps, up which the Brummie took his children to see the pets for sale in their cages. Somewhere within his inner ear the Brummie should hear the newsvendors' cry "Mail 'n' Despatch" and the croak of that old crone who shambled the city gutters urging him tunelessly to "Count his Blessings".

Our Brummie still has occasional lapses of vocabulary. The canal becomes the "cut", for all that his mother thought the word vulgar. The road becomes the "horse-road". He played in it as a boy; rolled marbles along its gutters uncluttered by cars, smote his tipcat across it, collected buckets of manure from it, clung to the backs of carts himself or shouted "Whip behind" to the driver if he saw another boy hanging on.

He knew, if the road was covered with bark from a nearby tannery, that this was to silence wheels passing a house with serious illness inside; and in days when caps were worn he always removed his and stood quietly as a funeral passed.

For childhood holidays our Brummie went to Rhyl or Blackpool, but he could have enjoyed a foretaste of the sea splashing through the early morning Fish Market in Bell Street en route for New Street Station with its hollow-sounding footbridge, one of his cherished institutions. He would have come to "town" by tramcar, and every pukka Brummie has travelled after dark on a topless

tram, hurling Jovian thunderbolts from the trolley-pole on the overhead wires. His other great tram ride was that Bank Holiday Lickey-bound romp on the Number 70 along Bristol Road's central reservation.

ABOVE. LIFFORD CANAL WHARF, OFF PERSHORE ROAD, ON WORCESTER AND BIRMINGHAM CANAL, WITH WORKING BOATS IN 1905. AT THE HUB OF BRINDLEY'S "CANAL CROSS," BIRMINGHAM HAD WATER LINKS WITH THE ESTUARIES OF THE MERSEY, HUMBER, THAMES AND SEVERN.

LEFT. CHRIST CHURCH LOOKED DOWN ON VICTORIA SQUARE FROM ITS COMPLETION IN 1815 UNTIL DEMOLISHED IN 1899 WHEN ITS CITY CENTRE CONGREGATION HAD MOVED TO THE INNER SUBURBS AND WERE ACCOMMODATED BY ST. AGATHA'S, SPARKBROOK, BUILT 1899-1901.

FAR LEFT. HANDSWORTH 1911. ONE OF BIRMINGHAM'S "TOPLESS" TRAMS. EVENTUALLY THE UPPER DECK WAS ROOFED WITH AN OPEN "BIRD-CAGE" AT EACH END.

In sporting nostalgia, where the Lancastrian cricket fan sighs for "my Hornby and my Barlow long ago", the Brummie has fond memories of his Calthorpe (the Hon. F.S.G.) and his Harry Howell in days when the Gentlemen and Players took the field at Edgbaston through different gates — and all the players were gentlemen! The Brummie could have seen Billy Quaife bowl unders to a nonplussed "Tiger" Smith as wicket-keeper.

▷

HOWEVER BIRMINGHAM HAS CHANGED OVER THE PAST CENTURY SINCE JOSEPH CHAMBERLAIN PUSHED CORPORATION STREET THROUGH A WARREN OF SLUMS FOR £34,000 IT HAS REMAINED BIRMINGHAM'S PRINCIPAL THOROUGHFARE. OUR PICTURES SHOW LEFT TO RIGHT. TOP 1892, 1914; AND BOTTOM 1946 AND 1950.

Just as his buildings, the Norwich Union, Beehive, High Street Co-op, the Grand and Royal theatres have given place to concrete uniformity, so have his cricketers in the anonymity of visored helmets, replacing those resplendent I.Zingari and Free Foresters caps.

The genuine Brummie remembers the "Blues" with a white V on their blue shirts. His heroes were Joe Bradford, Sam Hardy and Jesse Pennington. Geordies, Yorkshiremen and Cockneys have similar memories, but unique to the Brummie, his cap dripping rain on February afternoons, was the smoke from passing trains obliterating play at St. Andrew's. The Brummie is not a floodlight man — he recalls the flicker of smokers' matches on Spion Kop in December dusks.

Where the Brummie differed from other territorial counterparts was in the variety of "a thousand and one trades". Before the car and its accessories took over he worked in smaller communities. He knew his boss, a more approachable chap than those textile magnates up north. This may explain Birmingham's long Unionist allegiance prior to 1945 in Victoria Square and Westminster. The Brummie felt a pride in "Our Joe" no matter what he came eventually to think of Sir Austen and Neville.

Our Brummie's ancestry is a strange mixture of riotous High and Low Church mobs and of tolerance — to Welsh Quakers like the Lloyds, and Unitarians such as the Chamberlain-Martineau-Kenrick "clique" to which the city owes so much.

Bosley's pie shop; that famed trio of pubs, the White Horse, Congreve Street; the Hope and Anchor, Edmund Street; and the Woodman, Easy Row — Cannon Hill Park bandstand on summer Saturday evenings listening to the Police Band, with the sunlit boating lake shimmering through the trees. These all help make the Brummie, as did the "Monkey Run" when main streets teemed each night with well-behaved youngsters chatting and courting.

But now, diluted by easier travel, the Brummie we knew is dying. A new environment will breed a new 21st Century Brummie, moulded by the National Exhibition Centre, the International Airport, the Super Prix, the International Convention Centre, Pebble Mill, and the Pallasades. Only the accent will remain, the unchanging attribute of a changing Brummie. ◇ ◇ ◇

ABOVE. NELSON'S STATUE, IDENTIFIABLE TO THE DISCERNING BRUMMIE EYE IN THIS BULL RING OF 1950, WITH ITS VISTA DOWN JAMAICA ROW TO THE RIGHT OF ST. MARTIN'S. IN 1959 NELSON WAS REMOVED, TO BE UNVEILED AGAIN IN NOVEMBER 1961 NEAR MOOR STREET STATION.

LEFT. CANNON HILL PARK BOATING LAKE 1900 IS STILL A POPULAR BIRMINGHAM ATTRACTION.

Wragge & Co.

meeting the challenges of today's world backed with a tradition that spans 155 years

The Solicitors' practice of Wragge & Co., was founded in 1834 by George Wragge and Clement Ingleby. By the time Birmingham became a City in 1889 the practice was well established and had gained a reputation for meeting the challenges created by the rapid growth of industry and commerce in the Midlands. Many of those early clients have grown into important international organisations and are still valued clients to this day.

Our Offices in 1889

Wragge & Co. has continued to expand and now employs over 250 staff and twenty five partners responsible for providing a comprehensive range of legal services to both public and private companies, professional organisations and institutions throughout the U.K. and Europe.

The firm is based in modern city centre offices and uses the latest in modern computing and communications technology – yet still maintains the long tradition of being friendly and approachable.

For further information please contact:

Wragge & Co

Wragge & Co., Solicitors, Bank House, 8 Cherry Street, Birmingham B2 5JY.
Telephone: 021-632 4131.

A MEMBER OF THE M5 GROUP OF INDEPENDENT LEGAL PRACTICES

Michael Elphick is *Boon* as Central's network drama enters its third successful series.

Blockbusters with Bob Holness continues its gold run as a top young person's programme.

LOCAL,

Central is one of Birmingham's biggest success stories.

From our base in the city centre we are a major force in the world television market with unrivalled achievements across every sphere of our activity.

network programming with contributions like Boon, Blockbusters and Spitting Image— all made in Birmingham.

Globally, we're now recognised as one of the world's most creative and professional programme-makers—a fact endorsed by the 130 awards won since 1982.

We're currently filming new dramas and

NATIONAL,

Eden's Lost: a brilliant debut from Central Films, our new wholly-owned subsidiary.

Shot on location in Australia, *Fields of Fire II* is set to emulate the worldwide success of the original series.

Locally, we're committed to providing viewers with the very best in regional programming.

Our news service is the most-watched on ITV, supported by features of award-winning quality like ECO and Venture.

Off-screen, we're

documentaries all over the world, forging links with other international media organisations such as National Geographic, the Australian Broadcasting Corporation and NHK of Japan.

Following our success in winning a 1987 Queen's

GLOBAL.

equally committed to the region, as a major supporter and sponsor of community initiatives from Project Fullemploy in Birmingham and Coventry to B19, a unique inner-city drama project.

Nationally, we're the largest seven-day ITV company and a major supplier of top-rated

Award for Export Achievement, we've set up Central Television Enterprises (CTE) to market our programmes world-wide.

We are already building co-production links with France and Spain and are ready to exploit the broadcast revolution in Europe up to and after 1992.

Locally, nationally and globally. Central, a world-beater based in Birmingham.

CENTRAL.

Reagan bows out with perhaps his greatest tribute ever—a *Spitting Image* special.

Central Independent Television plc,
Central House, Broad Street, Birmingham B1 2JP. Tel: 021-643 9898

City of sport.

Birmingham, the leisure centre of Britain.

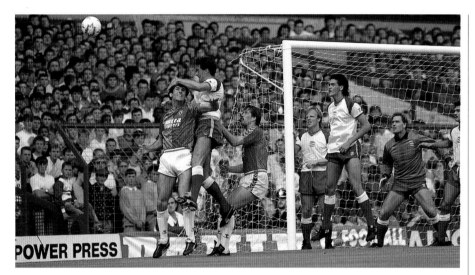

ABOVE. ASTON VILLA ON THE ATTACK AGAINST OLD RIVALS BIRMINGHAM CITY AT VILLA PARK.

BELOW. ACTION AT VILLA PARK DURING THE EARLY 1950s. THE ARCHED STAND, REMEMBERED BY MANY FANS WITH ITS ADVERTISEMENT FOR A LOCAL BREWERY, HAS BEEN REPLACED AND THE GROUND EXTENSIVELY MODERNISED.

The background to sport in Birmingham is so often the story of places and venues rather than just personalities.

The name of Aston Villa Football Club is known all over the globe, and as founder-members of the Football League the club has a history rich in honours and memories. Villa now play on a pitch surrounded by magnificent facilities, but actually started life on a ground just across the way, in Aston Park. They could not, however, claim exclusive use of that ground.

Cricket was also popular there, thousands turned out to see W. G. Grace perform, and the Australians beat England in under five hours on the same pitch. H.L. Cortis, a famous cyclist demonstrated the art of riding his 60 inch cycle and there was even lacrosse, played by a visiting team of Iroquois Indians.

It soon became obvious that Villa needed a more enclosed ground, with less competition for space, and by 1889 they were installed on a ground in Wellington Road, Perry Barr, on land let to them by a butcher for £5 a year. The players had to move a hayrick from the pitch before each game and there was a large hump near one goal. They changed in a blacksmith's hut.

The Perry Barr ground hosted several important games. The Amateur International between England and Ireland was staged there in February 1893, but a few years later

Villa were disqualified from the F.A. Cup when a tie against Preston was halted by a pitch invasion due mainly to over-crowding. There were 27,000 people in the Stadium, and Villa were found guilty of failing to maintain order. In the mid 1890's the lower grounds in Aston Park had been developed and Cup Semi-Finals had been played there so it was natural that the club should return. In 1897 Aston Villa was re-established in Aston and was now the strongest in the country.

Villa have been Division One champions seven times, and won the F.A. Cup on seven occasions. They were European Cup winners in 1981/2. There have been dark days too, relegation to Division Two has been accepted with patience by the fans several times, but the unthinkable happened in 1970 when the famous old club slipped into Division Three. Now back in the First Division under the dynamic leadership of Graham Taylor, Villa are once more emerging as a force in English Football.

Birmingham City, too, developed as a senior club in the 1890's playing as Small Heath Alliance at a ground in Muntz Street. The club was the first to become a limited liability company in football, taking the step at a time when there were crowds of just under 30,000 attending the matches.

In 1905 a change of the club name to Birmingham coincided with a move to Saint Andrews. Birmingham City have found honours hard to come by over the years. The championship of the Second Division and a Football League Cup win in 1963 is about the sum total of success, though a claim can be made to have helped establish the U.E.F.A. Cup, having played in its formative years as the 'Inter-Cities Fairs Cup'.

Amateur players, as such, no longer exist in soccer, the old ideal of the true amateur being replaced by 'non-contract' players. Moor Green Football Club founded in 1901 and based in Shirley was a bastion of the traditional amateur concept, but has now opted to play in the semi-professional Southern League.

Birmingham's Senior Rugby Club is one of the oldest in the country. Moseley celebrated its centenary in 1973, having represented the city at the highest level for the whole of its history. Traditional matches such as the one with Cardiff, have been played for a hundred years, except for the war years. The club has a fine ground at the Reddings, in Moseley, and has adapted to the demands of league rugby.

Birmingham Rugby Club plays at Portway, just outside the city, and has

survived a lean period on the field, culminating in relegation from the Third Division of the Leagues. Plans are underway to improve the standards.

The rise and decline of Birmingham Speedway over the years mirrors the changing fortunes of the sport itself. Brought to England sixty-one years ago speedway attracted huge crowds as riders such as Barry Briggs, Ivan Mauger and Ole Olsen became world champions. The Birmingham 'Brummies' had their own heroes. Graham Warren and George Major were stars and Hans Nielsen, later to become World Champion

brought thousands of people into Perry Barr in the later years of the track.

The team originally rode at a site on the Perry Barr ground near Birchfield Harriers, but when the team was re-established in recent seasons it rode at Perry Barr Greyhound Stadium. When that closed in 1984 the 'Brummies' moved briefly over the city to the 'Wheels' project, where a variety of sports on wheels were featured. An uneasy couple of seasons, sharing with hot rods and 'banger' racing followed before poor crowds and lack of general support caused the closure of the track once more. There are efforts being made to re-open on a site near the original one in Perry Barr. ▷

TOP LEFT. STRETCHING FOR IT AT THE REDDINGS – A MOSELEY LOCK-FORWARD WINS OUT EVEN THOUGH HE IS OUTNUMBERED.

BELOW. THE 1952 "BRUMMIES" AT PERRY BARR, WITH THE LEGENDARY GRAHAM WARREN. THE LINE-UP (BACK, LEFT TO RIGHT): GRAHAM WARREN, RON MOUNTFORD, ARTHUR PAYNE, RON MASON, IVOR DAVIES, LIONEL WATLING, GEOFF BENNETT. FRONT: ALAN HUNT, ERIC BOOTHROYD, BILL JEMISON, DAN FORSBURG.

BOTTOM. HANS NEILSEN LEADS BRUCE PENHALL IN A MATCH AT PERRY BARR.

The Edgbaston ground of Warwickshire County Cricket Club is a regular on the test cricket circuit, and the county club has been established for well over a hundred years. Three county championships have been won, as well as a Sunday league success in 1980. The Birmingham ground was the venue for the county's highest ever score, back in 1899

ABOVE. EDGBASTON, WARWICKSHIRE'S HOME GROUND EVEN THOUGH BIRMINGHAM IS NOT TECHNICALLY IN THE COUNTY. A LONGSTANDING VENUE FOR TEST CRICKET.

TOP RIGHT. JACK HOOD, BRITISH AND EUROPEAN WELTERWEIGHT CHAMPION.

BELOW. WARWICKSHIRE'S DENNIS AMISS CELEBRATES HIS 100th FIRST-CLASS CENTURY AT EDGBASTON IN 1986, AGAINST LANCASHIRE.

when Hampshire were hit for the mammoth total of 657 for 6 declared... Hampshire were also the victims in 1922 when Warwickshire bowled them out for just 15 runs. Dennis Amiss scored a total of 35,146 runs in a distinguished career at Edgbaston, and played 50 times for England. He represented the county for 27 years between 1960 and 1987. Commercially the county are one of the best in the country, with an organisation based at Edgbaston that runs as a huge business concern.

The city has boasted several well known boxers, starting well back in the 1850's with William Perry, the Tipton Slasher, who was based in Aston, later to become the focal point for so many sporting activities in the city. He was succeeded in the annals of Birmingham's pugilistic records by the great Jack Hood, who won the British Welterweight Title, and then went on to take the European version in controversial fashion. The year in question was 1933 and the venue, a famous

one in the city for boxing and wrestling, the Embassy Rink in Walford Road. Jack Hood was a firm favourite with his Birmingham public and met Stoker Reynolds for the British Title. Hood had earned the title in 1926, beating Harry Mason in London, and last defended it in 1928, in Birmingham, before making a triple attempt over two years to wrest the Middleweight Crown from Len Harvey. He lost two of those bouts and drew one and so returned to the Embassy to take on Stoker Reynolds for the lighter title. Hood turned in a superb display in front of a wildly enthusiastic home crowd. Reynolds was outclassed and eventually stopped in the ninth round. Just two months later the Birmingham man was in action again in the same Embassy Sportsdrome Ring. This time he was trying for the European Crown and he was clearly outpointing Adrien Aneet when the champion, from Belgium swung a desperate blow that landed low and was disqualified, much to his disgust but the delight of the Birmingham crowd. In all Jack Hood had 81 contests winning 66. In recent years Pat Cowdell has represented the city with distinction all over the world. He retired in 1988 after a career that saw him undefeated European Featherweight and Junior-Lightweight Champion.

He also held the British versions of both titles, and fought a magnificent fight against the great world champion Salvador Sanchez in Houston. Cowdell lost on a split points decision, but won many friends in the United States with his display. Cowdell fought many of his fights in the City, but the old Embassy was long since closed. The popular venue

now is the excellent Aston Villa Leisure Centre, and professional shows are also held at the Tower Ballroom in Edgbaston. Digbeth Civic Hall hosted many small shows and was usually packed, especially when the nearby market stallholders attended to see one of their ranks perform. Recent characters included Billy Baggott from the market, a slugging Light-Heavyweight, and Willie Wright, again from the ranks of the market boys, a Midlands Area Champion.

There is a fine tradition in Athletics in the city. The most famous name over the years has been Birchfield Harriers, with world record holder Peter Radford heading their team in the early sixties. Birchfield possessed a fine stadium in Perry Barr, but when that fell into disuse they were able to use the facilities at the new stadium just a few hundred yards away. The building by Birmingham City Council of this new home for Birmingham Athletics, 'The New Alexander Stadium' has led to the city stealing much of the thunder from Crystal Palace and Gateshead in international events. The annual programme of matches includes senior meetings against the likes of the United States and the German Democratic Republic, while recent years have also seen the staging of the European Junior Championships, and the National Schools

Championships, and as recently as August 1988, the Stadium played host to the biggest athletics event held in England for many years — the Olympic Trials.

Over the years while Birchfield have usually dominated the scene, clubs such as Small Heath A.C. and Sparkhill produced national class athletes, but Birchfield were the club which regularly provided international stars. One of the great memories from the heyday of Birchfield's original home — The Alexander Stadium, was the visit of Herb Elliott in October 1960. Over ten thousand people turned out to see him run and easily win over a world class field. That night was a 'one-off' for Birmingham athletics supporters. Nowadays the new stadium stages such nights frequently through the season.   ▷

TOP LEFT. MAJOR BOXING BOUTS NOW COME TO THE BIRMINGHAM INTERNATIONAL ARENA AT THE NEC.

TOP RIGHT. BRITAIN'S FIRST OLYMPIC TRIALS WERE HELD AT THE ALEXANDER STADIUM TO CHOOSE THE ATHLETICS TEAM FOR THE XXIV OLYMPIAD IN SEOUL, SOUTH KOREA IN 1988.

ABOVE THE NEW ALEXANDER STADIUM.

BELOW. FLASHBACK TO OCTOBER 1st 1960, WHEN THE AUSTRALIAN HERB ELLIOT RAN AT THE OLD ALEXANDER STADIUM.

Greyhound racing has figured in the sporting entertainment of the city over the years. At one stage tracks at Hall Green, Perry Barr and Kings Heath played hosts to thousands of punters, but as support dwindled so tracks lost money and the lure of cash from developers proved too strong to resist.

Kings Heath was the first track to go, closed in March 1971, and April 1984 saw Perry Barr follow, but Hall Green remains, having been in business since 1927. The track also provided a ground for "Hall Green Amateurs" Football Club, which enjoyed success in the sixties, but the club has since folded.

Leisure Centre, providing recreational swimming for thousands of people every week.

In recent years there have been two major developments in the sporting life of the city. An ambitious scheme to host the 1992 Olympics was approved by the National Olympic Committee over the claims of London and Manchester. The plans were to develop the facilities of the N.E.C., build an Athletes Village there as well as a 'Super-Stadium' and provide the best set-up of any Olympics.

The scheme brought worldwide acclaim to the city. It put the name of Birmingham on to the world sporting map, but Barcelona won the eventual vote. Nevertheless the city was well and truly established as a world leader where sport is concerned.

The N.E.C. has already housed top class boxing and indoor speedway. This year the European Skating Championships will be held there. Further efforts to secure major international sporting events for the city are being made.

In the 1970's the idea of a street race on the lines of the Monaco Grand Prix was mooted, but dismissed as unworkable, but after many years of work, and a successful plea by

As a new sport in this country, American Football strives to establish itself. The Birmingham Bulls are the leading team in England and have challenged the best in Europe. Matches have been played at the Salford Cycle Stadium and Birmingham Rugby Club and there is sufficient keenness to maintain the progress already made.

Swimming in the city has always been strong, with the schools leading that aspect of sport.

Woodcock Street Baths have supplied the training needs of thousands of young hopefuls over the years and now Olympian Nick Gillingham trains at Stechford. The City of Birmingham Swimming Club provided 5 members of the Olympic Team for the Seoul games.

The City Council provides over 20 swimming pools in the Birmingham area such as the brand new Cocks Moors Woods

TOP RIGHT. BIRMINGHAM'S FIRST PUBLIC SWIMMING BATHS WERE AT KENT STREET IN 1851. THE MODERN COCKS MOORS WOODS LEISURE CENTRE IS THE LATEST OF BIRMINGHAM'S POOLS.

BELOW RIGHT. THE LOGO OF BIRMINGHAM LEISURE.

ABOVE. BIRMINGHAM'S NEWEST TEAM SPORT, THE FAST-GROWING AMERICAN FOOTBALL, WITH THE TOP TEAM, THE BIRMINGHAM BULLS WHO WON THE BRITISH CHAMPIONSHIP PLAYOFF IN 1988.

TOP LEFT. THE NEC HOSTS THE 1989 EUROPEAN FIGURE-SKATING CHAMPIONSHIPS, THEIR FIRST APPEARANCE IN BRITAIN FOR 50 YEARS.

Birmingham City Council to Parliament to force through an Act to close the roads for two days each year, the race is now a reality. The "Halfords Birmingham Super Prix" is a two day festival on the streets of the city centre with a carnival atmosphere and two full packed days of entertainment as well as motor sport. The main race is the Formula 3,000, one step down from the full Grand Prix

cars. Stilt walkers and bands crowd the streets and the cars speed round a full Grand Prix Circuit close to the thousands of spectators who come from all over Europe to see the action. The next step is to go for a full Grand Prix and already plans are there to try for that goal.

The Birmingham Athletic Institute was established a hundred years ago in the city centre providing sport and recreation of all sorts for the people. Now its successor, the Birmingham Sports Centre is housed in plusher surroundings on the site of the Super Prix, just outside the city centre, still providing facilities for any resident who cares

to try sport. At grass roots level, Birmingham City Council continues to provide recreation and leisure facilities throughout the city. It

was over 100 years ago that the city fathers first opened a park for the enjoyment of the Birmingham public. Today, thousands of acres of parkland are the colourful 'home' for millions of flowers, shrubs and trees. The Council has established a comprehensive network of indoor sports and facilities — swimming pools, leisure centres and the new dual-use centres, a pioneering policy

whereby school recreation and community facilities are opened up to all local people. Birmingham also boasts some of the country's best municipal golf courses.

So Birmingham moves on, still striving to establish and spearhead sport into the next century. The spirit of the men who built Aston Villa, and brought European glory to the basic surroundings of the Embassy Hall still lives on in the plans of the people seeking to further promote Birmingham as a World Sporting Centre. ◇ ◇ ◇ ◇ ◇ ◇

ABOVE. ON THE GRID WITH THE START OF THE HALFORDS BIRMINGHAM SUPER PRIX. BRITAIN'S ONLY STREET RACING CIRCUIT.

BELOW. MR PERERA HOSTED THE FIRST RECORDED GAME OF LAWN TENNIS (LAWN RACKETS) AT HIS HOME IN AMPTON ROAD, EDGBASTON, IN 1866, THE GAME OF RACKETS OR FIVES WAS ALSO STARTED IN BIRMINGHAM IN 1833.

BOTTOM RIGHT. THERE ARE MORE THAN A QUARTER OF A MILLION ROUNDS OF GOLF PLAYED EVERY YEAR ON BIRMINGHAM CITY COUNCIL COURSES.

BOTTOM LEFT. BIRMINGHAM COUNCIL ENCOURAGES RESIDENTS TO TRY THEIR HANDS AT NEW SPORTS.

TOP LEFT. HALFORDS BIRMINGHAM SUPER PRIX WITH CARS TRAVELLING AT 140 MPH WHERE NORMALLY ONLY 40 MPH IS ALLOWED — IN THE OPPOSITE DIRECTION!

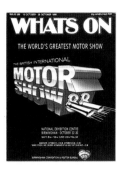

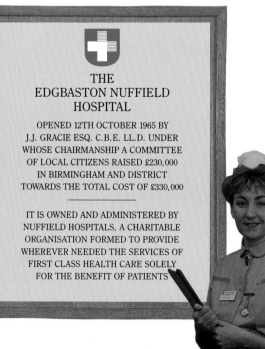

Congratulations on a great City's first century

The Pallasades wishes Birmingham and the people of Birmingham continuing prosperity and success.

Crucial
Decisions

Are your property consultants members of your corporate financial team? Do they buy and sell properties in every commercial sector, deal with individual investments as well as major portfolios, and arrange the funding of development projects? Are they involved in the creation of your investment strategy?

Be sure you have all the information and advice you need before making those crucial decisions.

We've always had independent views on Birmingham's development.

Elliott Son & Boyton, the independent property advisers have long been associated with many of Birmingham's finest property development activities covering Commercial, Industrial and Retail schemes. For further details of our range of activities contact us at the address below.

Elliott Son & Boyton

Surveyors, Valuers & Auctioneers
Established 1845

30 Waterloo Street, Birmingham B2 5TJ
Fax 021-200 2008 Telex 337769

021-200 2007

The Independent Property Advisers

B I R M I N G H A M • L O N D O N

For 268 years a cornerstone
of British insurance

Since 1720 GRE has been busily meeting the insurance needs of private individuals and companies around the world.

Through the years we've continually improved and expanded our range of services, combining the considerable skills of our own people with the most up-to-date technology available.

But by no means are we a stony-faced giant; in fact, we like to think we offer our customers insurance with a human touch.

Guardian Royal Exchange Plc. Midlands Area Office: 10 Temple Street, Birmingham B2 5BP.

City of welcome.

Birmingham, the international family.

The Birmingham community is wide, and can as well have links with the highrise waterfront of Hong Kong as the wheatfields of Warwickshire.

For the city of a thousand trades could not have grown without the contribution of people from all over the world who have made their homes in Birmingham.

The city's community reflects the tastes of a hundred different cultures.

Where else would Chinese Christians use a Welsh Presbyterian church for their meetings.

Where else, indeed might there be not one but three Welsh churches, but in a city whose vitality and prosperity are built on the rich cultures of a thousand different welcomes.

Warwickshire, Wales and Hong Kong represent just three of the roots of the city's million people, one fifth of them from the Commonwealth, with a substantial leavening of Welsh, Irish, Scots and East Europeans, particularly Poles.

For it has long been a magnet of opportunity, from the days when it was first granted its market charter, through the Industrial Revolution, the Hungry Thirties and the post-war boom.

This is the community that Birmingham City Council and its forebears set out to serve in 1889.

This is the community which the Council serves today, albeit in different ways, and will continue to serve in the next century.

And serve, no doubt, in different ways in the future as the nature of local government changes.

The spirit of municipal enterprise which characterised the Birmingham of 1889 and the years after is as lively as ever, though its objectives have changed with national changes in the concept of local government.

The city which set out directly to provide its citizens with police, fire, water, gas, electricity and public transport has seen these functions taken into wider control, or even returned to private ownership.

Gas and electricity were nationalised in

TOP LEFT. THE WEST MIDLANDS AMBULANCE SERVICE IN ACTION AT BIRMINGHAM INTERNATIONAL AIRPORT.

TOP CENTRE. WEST MIDLANDS POLICE, LEADS THE WAY IN COMMUNITY POLICING AND ACTIVELY ENCOURAGES THE RECRUITMENT OF BLACK OFFICERS.

THE BADGE OF THE WEST MIDLANDS FIRE SERVICE.

BOTTOM LEFT. CARNIVAL TIME IN HANDSWORTH, THE ALL SINGING, ALL DANCING CALYPSO PARTY, THE BIRMINGHAM CARNIVAL, IS THE SECOND LARGEST OF ITS TYPE IN BRITAIN.

BOTTOM CENTRE. THE CHINESE NEW YEAR CELEBRATIONS BRING THE MAGIC OF THE ORIENT TO THE STREETS OF BIRMINGHAM.

BOTTOM RIGHT. THE ELAN VALLEY AQUEDUCT, BRINGING FRESH WELSH WATER TO BIRMINGHAM.

1948; gas was placed into shareholders hands in 1986, and electricity is to follow.

Water was taken into wider public ownership under the Severn Trent Water Authority in 1974, and is about to return to the private sector.

Police, fire and public transport, where the city has a long and honourable tradition, became part of wider West Midlands bodies in 1974 with the creation of West Midlands County Council.

That body became responsible for strategic planning, waste disposal, highways and Birmingham International Airport.

Its abolition in 1986 saw the creation of joint boards of the seven local authorities in the former county council area to continue to operate the joint services.

Birmingham International Airport has become a public limited company, although the shares are all in local authority hands.

The local authority-owned buses were placed in the hands of a public limited company, West Midlands Travel, with the deregulation of bus services in 1986, though transport strategy remains in the hands of the local authorities through the West Midlands Passenger Transport Authority.

This authority is responsible for promoting the Midland Metro, a new railborne transport system designed in part to encourage economic regeneration of the Birmingham Heartlands area and the Black Country.

The changes emphasise the changing concept of local government.

In essence the City Council is able to concentrate more on providing for the personal and economic well-being of its citizens.

The City Council is pushing hard for economic regeneration, particularly of the inner city, with the object of tackling unemployment.

A wide range of incentives and support are promoted, to encourage new and traditional industry, and a successful campaign is being waged to promote "Made in Birmingham" as a label of proud craftmanship.

Educational provision is wide-ranging, with vocational training a key element long before it became identified as a vital national priority.

Adult education is an important element; any company in Birmingham can send its adult workers to college for retraining.

Birmingham Polytechnic also caters for adults with 6,000 full-time and 5,000 part-time places.

The century-old institution has recently gained the right to give its senior tutors the title Professor.

Community care goes to the grassroots, with Community Health Councils as the consumer watchdogs, ensuring that the pressures of financial constraints and staff shortages, endemic in some areas of the NHS, do not avoidably affect patient care.

The city's social services department plays a major role especially in child care and services for the elderly and the disabled.

The city is extending consultation and contact with its citizens through a network of area sub-committees and neighbourhood offices.   ▷

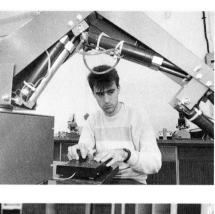

TOP LEFT. WEST MIDLANDS TRAVEL BUSES IN CORPORATION STREET PROVIDING TRANSPORT FOR MILLIONS.

TOP RIGHT. ENGINEERING STUDIES AT BIRMINGHAM POLYTECHNIC, THE LARGEST IN THE COUNTRY.
BOTTOM LEFT. MIDLANDS METRO'S FIRST LINE WILL BE OPEN IN 1992, USING ELECTRIC RAILCARS TO LINK BIRMINGHAM WITH THE BLACK COUNTRY AND WOLVERHAMPTON

ABOVE: NACHDEY HASDEY GROUP 'PUNJAB' DANCE

They provide yet another link and point of contact for services such as housing, leisure, environment and planning.

Birmingham has more than 40 hospitals run by five separate health districts, with fine facilities and an enviable record for medical innovation.

The Queen Elizabeth Medical Centre is the focal point, based near Birmingham University.

Here the Queen Elizabeth Hospital, opened in 1938 and celebrating the 50th anniversary of its royal dedication in 1989, is alongside Birmingham Maternity Hospital and the university medical school.

Over the years, black and brown faces have appeared in councillors' seats in the Council Chamber and been hailed as a

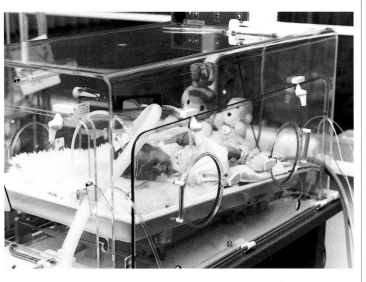

TOP RIGHT. RABBI SINGER CONDUCTS A TALMUD TORAH CLASS AT THE CENTRAL SYNAGOGUE.
ABOVE. CARE FROM THE CRADLE IN BIRMINGHAM'S HOSPITALS.

further breakthrough in the field of race relations.

In fact Birmingham had its first Asian councillor in the 1940s when the late Dr. Dhani Prem was elected.

Its many religious communities add to the tapestry.

The tightly-knit Jewish community — the first Jewish settler in the city was one Aron Moses who lived in the Froggery, the area behind New Street, as far back as 1780 — supports four synagogues and King David's School, a primary school for Jewish children.

Who can fail to have noticed the huge dome of the Central Mosque in Belgrave Middleway, its minaret adding a touch of the East to the city skyline, which is just the tip of Birmingham's Islamic iceberg.

Its size is second only to the Regent's Park Mosque in London and its catchment area is the Midlands.

But mosques can be any size.

Moslems from certain villages will congregate for prayers in private homes, and they are building more formal places of worship.

At Birchfield, Perry Barr, for instance, the President Saddaam Hussein Mosque rears its dome within yards of Holy Trinity Church.

And who can fail to appreciate the West Indian adaptations of worship exported to their native islands.

These have become 78 small churches where, on Sundays, black worshippers raise the roofs with sacred music, pay a tithe (one tenth) of their income to support their pastor — often a working man through the week — and live strictly by the Bible.

The Mount Beulah chapels, the Shiloh United Church of Christ Apostolic, The Life and Light Fellowship, and the rest, draw in one fifth of all black people in Birmingham.

Birmingham's Roman Catholics have long had their own cathedral, Augustus Pugin's St Chad's, the first to be built in post-reformation Britain, on what is now St Chad's Queensway.

They have their own Archbishop and they have their claim to a place in the ecclesiastical history books with the stewardship of Cardinal John Henry Newman who founded the Oratory of St Philip Neri; the Italian Renaissance basilica in Hagley Road is Edwardian.

Eastern Orthodoxy has a base at St Lazar's, the Serbian Orthodox church in Bournville, the only European building of its type outside Yugoslavia and only completed in all its Byzantine glory in 1968.

But nonconformism was the spring of Birmingham's radicalism and the inspiration for its founding fathers.

Chamberlain himself was a Unitarian, and George Dawson and Robert Dale ministers, the latter at the Carrs Lane church whose site and spirit survive.

Many chapels and churches have been adapted to the religions of the Commonwealth immigrants, particularly the various sects from the Indian sub-continent.

Birmingham was a target for Anglican churchbuilding in the Victorian period.

But churches like St. Paul's in Hockley and St. Philip's which became the Anglican cathedral in 1905, were the result of the expansion of the population in the period before and during the Industrial Revolution.

The churches are the most noticeable manifestations of Birmingham's many cultures, along with the streets of Handsworth, Ladywood, Balsall Heath, Sparkbrook and the burgeoning Chinese quarter off Smallbrook Queensway.

The accents of the long-time Brummies mingle with the Celtic voices of workers whose forebears a couple of generations ago came from the mines to work in the car factories.

After them came the Commonwealth immigrants from the West Indies, Africa, the Indian sub-continent and the Far East to work in all modes of life, rebuilding the city after 1945.

The city is a refuge for those who have fled from famine, war and oppression in other parts of the world.

Perhaps the City of a Thousand Trades should be changed to "a City of a thousand welcomes and customs." ◇ ◇ ◇ ◇

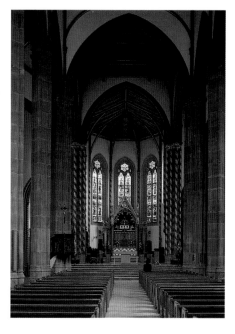

TOP LEFT. THE BIRMINGHAM CENTRAL MOSQUE, SECOND LARGEST IN BRITAIN, THE MUEZZIN CAN USE THE MINARET TO SUMMON MOSLEMS TO PRAYER.

TOP RIGHT. ST. CHAD'S PUGIN'S VICTORIAN-GOTHIC REVIVAL OF 1841 CONTAINS 16th CENTURY FLEMISH AND GERMAN ARTS, AND WINDOWS BY JOHN HARDMAN OF BIRMINGHAM SHOW HOW STAINED GLASS IS MADE.

BOTTOM RIGHT. ST. PHILIP'S CATHEDRAL, BUILT IN 1715 BY A WILLIAM SHAKESPEARE TO THOMAS ARCHER'S DESIGN, NAMED AFTER ROBERT PHILLIPS WHO DONATED THE LAND. STAINED GLASS BY BURNE-JONES AND CENTRE OF THE BIRMINGHAM DIOCESE SINCE 1905.

BOTTOM LEFT. ST. LAZAR'S, BYZANTIUM COME TO BIRMINGHAM, CENTRE FOR EASTERN ORTHODOXY, COMPLETED IN 1968.

WEST MIDLANDS FIRE SERVICE

SMOKE KILLS!

Every year nearly 60,000 fires occur in the home in this country alone, killing about 700 people and injuring over 70,000 others. A lot of these deaths and injuries might have been prevented if only the people involved had been able to escape before it was too late. Smoke detectors can give you the extra time that is necessary.

Smoke detectors don't stop fires and they can't put them out, but if they are properly installed and looked after they can give you an early warning of fire and increase your chances of escape.

SMOKE DETECTORS SAVE LIVES FIT THEM NOW

ASK YOUR LOCAL FIRE STATION FOR INFORMATION

WE'VE COME A LONG WAY IN
THE LAST HUNDRED YEARS...

(Now for
the next)

In the days of the horse drawn corporation bus and tram, the very idea of a motorised bus was beyond imagination.

To the passengers of 1888, today's streamlined vehicles would have seemed like a vision from science fiction; the idea that one could travel from Birmingham to London in just two and a half hours a mere flight of fancy! But possible it certainly is on London Liner, West Midlands Travel's luxury Birmingham to London coach service.

Today, West Midlands Travel moves a staggering 1½ million people 220,000 miles every day. There are Timesavers, the fast town to town service, minibuses for local travel, and of course standard double and single deckers taking you where you want to go, when you want to go – and back again.

Yesterday's dreams are today's reality. And if we can come so far in one hundred years what will the next century have in store?

Like the people of the nineteenth century, we can but speculate.

One thing, however, is certain. The travellers of tomorrow can be sure to enjoy the high standards of service and reliability that we're setting today at West Midlands Travel.

West Midlands Travel Limited,
16 Summer Lane, Birmingham B19 3SD
Telephone 021-236 8313.

WAKE UP TO THE FUTURE

THE GALLERIES
AT THE BULL RING

London & Edinburgh Trust PLC - one of the most innovative, resourceful and successful property companies in the United Kingdom - is investing in excess of £250 million in Birmingham's future.

The total redevelopment of the Bull Ring Shopping Centre is proposed and LET is to create The Galleries at the Bull Ring, a prestigious three level centre comprising one million square feet of shopping.

The major aspects of the scheme include:

- a major department store on three levels
- four large anchor stores on two levels
- 175 smaller shops ranging from banks and building societies to speciality foodshops, patisseries and confectioners, including a range of restaurants and fast-food outlets
- all shopping under cover
- access to each level by lifts and escalators from a number of points along the mall
- parking for some 3,500 cars with direct access to the shopping centre
- seating in the malls; public conveniences and public telephones
- 5,000 new jobs for local people

LONDON & EDINBURGH TRUST PLC

BELIEVING IN BIRMINGHAM

City of attractions.

Birmingham, the big heart of England.

ABOVE. BIRMINGHAM HAS MORE MILES OF CANALS THAN VENICE, AND THEY HAVE BEEN TRANSFORMED FROM GRIMY WORKING WATERWAYS TO CHANNELS OF RECREATION. FARMER'S BRIDGE LOCKS ARE STILL A CHALLENGE TO BOATMEN.

RIGHT. HALFORDS BIRMINGHAM SUPER PRIX, FEATURES DRIVERS FROM A DOZEN NATIONS FOR A TWO-DAY FESTIVAL OF RACING AND ENTERTAINMENT.

Every August Bank Holiday the streets just off the city centre are closed to hold a motor race and Birmingham echoes to the roar of highly tuned car engines and the squeal of tyres.

The Halfords Birmingham Super Prix is a round of the international Formula 3000 series, using cars just a stage removed from Grand Prix racers.

The event and the street racing festival surrounding it are part of an initiative by the City Council to book a firm place for Birmingham on the tourist map.

The International Convention Centre which is rising on a site just off the city centre is another part of that venture, aimed at boosting business tourism.

The £121 million development will open in 1991, and may help to revive the Birmingham tradition for political discussion, with the major political parties and trade unions bringing their annual conferences to the city.

Tourism is a major development target for Birmingham City Council.

The first recorded tourist was the Royal Commissioner John Leland in 1536, sent around the country by Henry VIII to report on the likely sources of materials for the wars against France.

It was a time when travel was limited to the few who struggled along the rutted roads of the Middle Ages and who would hardly consider themselves as tourists in the modern sense.

Leland and others who followed down the centuries seemed in awe of the industrial progress they found in a town which may well be in the centre of England, but suffered all the problems of getting its goods to a wider market.

Canals, railways, motorways and air travel have in their turn changed the situation dramatically, shrinking the world and, together with wider affluence, boosting the desire and ability to travel.

So was born the modern tourist, though tradition still considers them unlikely to want to reverse the flow and visit a major commercial city.

The examples of other grim industrial cities show the opposite is possible, for there is still a heritage to promote however much it has been ignored in the name of progress.

So Birmingham has taken up the challenge of tourism.

For tourism means money, money means jobs, jobs in service industry to replace those which have gone from manufacturing and which will never return in the numbers once known, and Birmingham wants its slice of the tourist cake.

The founders of modern Birmingham took great pains to make sure there were parks and gardens to attract the citizens, and Aston Fields, the grounds of Aston Hall, became a major pleasure attraction, the Alton Towers of its day.

Sutton Park became Birmingham's largest green lung.

Visitors to Birmingham can now take a sightseeing tour on an open-top bus, and travel more easily on the city's miles of canals,

more than there are in Venice.

They can see the hidden gem of the Jacobean Aston Hall, visit the industrial heritage at Sarehole Mill, smell steam and hot oil at Birmingham Railway Museum, visit the Art Gallery built on the profits of the corporation gas works, complete with its collection of Pre-Raphaelite paintings. ▷

TOP LEFT. SAREHOLE MILL, AT SWANSHURST ON THE RIVER COLE, USED FOR GRINDING CORN, THEN AS A BLADE MILL, DERELICT IN 1919, NOW RESTORED TO WORKING ORDER.

TOP RIGHT. BIRMINGHAM RAILWAY MUSEUM, TYSELEY, ON THE SITE OF A FORMER ENGINE SHED, A MAJOR CENTRE FOR RESTORING AND PRESERVING THE RAILWAY HERITAGE.

ABOVE. THE GREAT HALL, GRAND ENTRANCE OF ASTON HALL, BUILT BY SIR THOMAS HOLTE.

RIGHT. INVITATION TO A ROYAL VISIT, 1858, WHEN QUEEN VICTORIA OPENED ASTON HALL AND ITS PARK TO THE PUBLIC.

LEFT. SAILING ON THE LAKE IN SUTTON PARK. BIRMINGHAM HAS MORE THAN 6,000 ACRES OF PARKLAND AND OPEN SPACES.

They can take a world gastronomical tour in the city's restaurants, from the tradition of English roast beef, through Europe to the wonders of North and South America and the spices of the Orient, never forgetting the relish of the Caribbean.

TOP LEFT. THE BARTONS ARMS, ASTON, RESTORED VICTORIAN PUBLIC HOUSE.

TOP RIGHT. THE PAVILIONS SHOPPING CENTRE IN BIRMINGHAM HAS WON AN INTERNATIONAL AWARD AS EUROPE'S BEST NEW SHOPPING DEVELOPMENT.

ABOVE. CARIBBEAN COOKING AND CARIBBEAN HOSPITALITY BY RUSTIE LEE.

BOTTOM RIGHT. THE JEWELLERY QUARTER, HOCKLEY; CONSERVATION AREA AND HOME OF MANUFACTURING AND RETAIL JEWELLERS.

They can shop in one of Birmingham's impressive shopping centres including the international award-winning Pavilions and the City Plaza. They can visit the famous Bull Ring Centre — the first shopping centre of its kind in the country when it opened in the 60's and now to be redeveloped to meet the needs of City shoppers in the 90's.

They can use the city's burgeoning hotels as a base for exploring further afield.

The International Convention Centre will attract not only business people, but their partners who will be offered associated guided tours.

In the Industrial Revolution, the factory owners would invite visitors, proud to show off the new processes they had invented.

Lord and Lady Shelburne visited Birmingham in 1766, and each left their own account of the visit.

Lady Shelburne concentrated on the people:

May 15   We got into the coach for Birmingham and arrived through rough roads at 9 o'clock there, We were kindly and politely received by Mr. Garbett.

Went with Mr. Garbett to see the manufacturers of buttons and hardwares which are very curious, Mr. Taylor, the principal manufacturer dined with us and we went after to Mr. Boulton's who trades in the same way. His house is a very pretty one about a mile out of town and his workshops newly built at the end of his garden where they take up a large piece of ground which he has named Soho Square. There, as in the morning, we purchased some watch chains and trinkets at an amazing cheap price and drank tea afterwards at his house which is a very pleasant one.

May 16   This morning we went to Mr. Gimlett's where we bought a great many toys and saw his warehouse of watches etc., one of which I bought for Master Parker. We also went to a Quakers to see the making of guns...

We went in a coach to Mr. Baskerville's which is a pretty place out of the town. He showed us his garden and a hot house and Mrs. Baskerville showed us the Japan Works because she had chiefly the management of it.

His Lordship's account is much more down to earth, describing the way the manufacturers of buttons and toys divided the tasks among the workers, down to children of six years old, and the development of trade with the Colonies.

Elkington's electro-plating factory in Newhall Street was thrown open to all to see its revolutionary processes, patented in 1840.

Nowadays visitors can see revolutionary

car-making at Austin Rover's Longbridge car factory.

And by a strange quirk of fate, they can still go to Elkington's, because the former factory houses the Birmingham Museum of Science and Industry.

The city boasts the largest Lyric theatre in the country and two other major theatres besides, plus restaurants, night clubs and all the trappings for a night out.

And it has the City of Birmingham Symphony Orchestra, whose permanent conductor, Simon Rattle, has firmly resisted tempting offers elsewhere.

The International Convention Centre will provide the orchestra with a new home.

It will also form an adjunct to the National Exhibition Centre at Bickenhill, over the city's boundary in the neighbouring borough of Solihull.   ▷

TOP LEFT. CAR-MAKING BY ROBOTS AT LONGBRIDGE, HOME OF AUSTIN ROVER.

BELOW. NIGHT CLUB CITY... THE DOME, HORSEFAIR.

BOTTOM. THE CLIMAX OF THE MILK RACE IN BIRMINGHAM, THE SPECTACULAR ROUND BRITAIN INTERNATIONAL CYCLE TOUR.

LEFT. THE LAST OF ENGLAND,' PAINTED BY FORD MADOX BROWN IN 1855.
REPRODUCED BY PERMISSION OF THE BIRMINGHAM MUSEUM AND ART GALLERY.

The NEC was Birmingham's coup of the 1970s, built against the scepticism of an exhibition industry accustomed in Britain only to the confines of Earl's Court and Olympia in London.

The NEC aimed higher, emulating the great showgrounds of the Continent and succeeding in staging since then all but the biggest peripatetic events.

The NEC has gained international recognition for Birmingham by staging events such as the British International Motor Show, the international machine tool exhibition, and other major trade shows.

These exhibitions put to the test one of the NEC's marketing attractions, Birmingham International Airport, alongside the NEC and with a main railway line to London in between them.

The airport is already extending the £60 million new terminal with a £35 million programme to extend the terminal building and provide runway improvements and extra equipment.

Passenger traffic is expected to rise to 5 million by 1992.

The NEC will stage more than 100 exhibitions in 1989, a far cry from its opening year when it staged a mere dozen.

TOP. INTERNATIONAL SUPERSTAR DIANA ROSS AT THE BIRMINGHAM INTERNATIONAL ARENA, A MAJOR VENUE ON THE CONCERT CIRCUIT.
RIGHT. THE BRITISH INTERNATIONAL MOTOR SHOW, EVERY TWO YEARS A MOTOR INDUSTRY SHOP WINDOW AT THE NEC.
ABOVE. BLAKESLEY HALL, A PRIME EXAMPLE OF ELIZABETHAN ARCHITECTURE.

Its spectacular tent-like Arena with its pillar-free space is home for pop concerts, horse shows and the British Telecom and British Gas annual meetings.

It is the only site in the country able to accommodate the potential number of shareholders who wish to attend.

In Birmingham's Centenary Year it stages the European Figure Skating Championships, the first time they have come to Britain in 50 years.

The NEC is the main centre of Birmingham's bid for a major international sporting event such as the Olympics, Commonwealth or European Games, and development continues as it has done since the centre first opened in 1976.

The aim is to double its floor space to 200,000 sq. metres and the first 20,000 sq. metres which open in Birmingham's Centenary Year are part of a £40 million building programme to the North East of the present halls.

In Centenary Year also the NEC hosts its second major international convention, after Rotary International used the site in 1984, bringing 23,000 delegates.

That will be the 44th JCI World Congress, with thousands of Jaycees from more than 100 countries.

Even that sort of event may be beyond the capacity of the International Convention Centre, which is firmly aimed at the business convention market.

The International Convention Centre will comprise eleven sophisticated halls around a spectacular Mall, designed to provide the most advanced and complete range of facilities that any meeting planner could possibly need for conferences from 30 to 3,000 delegates.

There is seating for 1,500 in the main conference hall, which has a huge stage and flytower.

The concert hall has been designed with world-class acoustics for the 2,200 capacity audience.

It will be set out in the traditional "shoe box" style of the great 19th Century concert halls such as the Musikverein in Vienna, and will be a fitting new home for the City of Birmingham Symphony Orchestra, which is also being consulted closely on the design.

Part of the development will be available as a mini convention centre for the smaller meetings, with a separate entrance and facilities.

A Mall forms the focal point of the development, and sub-meeting rooms or "breakout" suites are planned for smaller sessions of major conferences.

The centre is also marketing the proposed national indoor sports arena, which will be built in the vicinity with a conference capacity of 8,000 when not used as a much-needed running track. Alongside will be a festival marketplace modelled on the famous Baltimore scheme, including aquarium and Omnimax cinema.

The target for the centre is a slice of the UK conference market, presently worth about £1,000 million a year.

Those conferences attracted 213,000 overseas visitors in the past year, spending more than £470 a head during their stay.

Part of the convention centre development includes a major hotel which is to be the flagship of the Hyatt hotel chain.

Tourism is a growing industry, far removed from commerce and industry, but an example of the flair shown by Birmingham entrepreneurs, ever willing to grasp a new opportunity. ◇ ◇ ◇ ◇ ◇

TOP. INTERNATIONAL CONVENTION CENTRE, THE CENTRAL MALL.

ABOVE. A LOOK TO 1991: HOW THE INTERNATIONAL CONVENTION CENTRE AND HYATT HOTEL WILL TRANSFORM THE VIEW DOWN BROAD STREET.

BOTTOM LEFT. SIMON RATTLE, PRINCIPAL CONDUCTOR OF THE WORLD RENOWNED CITY OF BIRMINGHAM SYMPHONY ORCHESTRA.

Publishers for
The City of Birmingham
The Birmingham Convention & Visitor Bureau
The Heart of England Tourist Board
The National Exhibition Centre

New Enterprise Publications Limited, 212 Broad Street, Birmingham B15 1AY.
Telephone: 021-643 8921. Fax: 021-633 3119

WINNER OF EUROPE'S INTERNATIONAL

SHOPPING CENTRE AWARD 1988.

WHERE YOU CAN BE IN STYLE

WITHOUT BEING OUT OF POCKET.

PAVILIONS
HIGH STREET   *BIRMINGHAM*
IT'S YOUR KIND OF SHOPPING

Ever since our first apprentice worked one of the original single-colour Thompson Presses back in 1947 . . .

KNP, (then known as Kings Norton Press Ltd) has striven on to become one of the UK's leading Independent Colour Printers, this claim being fully justified in 1987, when, on our 40th birthday we were presented with the *'Printer of the Year'* Award.

Understandably we're proud of our history and proud also to be associated with Birmingham, as we offer our warmest congratulations on this, the city's Centenary Year. Undoubtedly Birmingham's central location and local workforce have been a major influence on our success.

Thankfully, production methods have changed considerably since 1947, but the basic KNP principles have, and always will, remain the same. We pride ourselves on keeping in the fore-front of technology in Design, Reproduction, Print and Finishing, yet always maintaining the highest standards of Service, Quality, Honesty and as the last 40 years have shown, Reliability.

It is with our Scitex repro system, Heidelberg sheet fed and web presses and a continuing policy of investing in the future, that we look forward to our own Centenary: perhaps with as much confidence and enthusiasm as did that first apprentice.

*Oxleasow Road
East Moons Moat
Redditch B98 0RE*

Quality Produced
Quality Rewarded

A complete professional service . . . All under one roof